Soul Connection

Ayderline
the spirit within

by Sharon Milne Barbour

Soul Connection - Ayderline the spirit within

Copyright © 2017 by Sharon Milne Barbour

Published by Bengalrose Healing

Designed by Sharon Milne Barbour

Author - Sharon Milne Barbour

Book cover illustration – by Chris Barbour from www.cimbart.co.uk

All rights are reserved. No part of this book may be reproduced by any mechanical, photographic, or electrical process, or in the form of a phonographic recording, nor may it be stored in a retrieval system, transmitted, or otherwise be copied for public or private use - other than for "fair use" as brief quotations embodied in articles or spiritual services credited to Bengalrose. Reviews not to be written without prior written knowledge of the publisher and author. The intent of the author is only to offer information of a general nature to help you on your spiritual path. In the event you use any of the information in the book for yourself, which are your right, the author and the publisher assumes no responsibility for your actions.

CONTENTS

Soul connection – spirit within

Chapter 1	Hello, beautiful Earth!	10
Chapter 2	Spirit within Alexander - *Earth*	33
Chapter 3	Spirit within Ylva - *Earth*	56
Chapter 4	Spirit within Eliza – *Earth*	69
Chapter 5	Spirit within Marceline - *Earth*	84
Chapter 6	Spirit within Isliquine - *Castrolian*	101
Chapter 7	A guide to Harry - *Earth*	119
Chapter 8	Spirit within Sharon - *Earth*	132
Chapter 9	Discover your true self	162
	About the author	178

Soul connection – spirit within

My name is Ayderline and this is the story of my incarnated life's and spirit guide experiences. I am going to take you on a journey through time and dimensions, enabling you to experience with me some of my physical incarnated lives. I begin my story in my home world before I travel to Earth to ancient Greece, at the time of the end of the Roman Empire. My incarnated Earth lives and experiences take you to the Viking period, the age of Napoleon, England's green farmlands, the Second World War and then as far as your modern day. Along the way, I will share my experiences of dying from a broken heart, the fear of war, love, survival and heartache. As well as all this, you will be taken on a journey to another planet and be part of my physical existence as a highly evolved ascension being.

You all on Earth have a spirit within or, as some of you call it, a soul. Many humans live their lives unaware of the soul and higher self-connections. You will find great joy if you learnt to connect to this love source of divine energy. The spirit within stays with you as part of your life's journey, guiding you forward on your life's path – it is your sat-nav through life. Your spirit within might be on its first visit to a physical being incarnation existence, or they might have lived many physical lives already on various planets; please remember the Earth saying: *"They have an old soul."* There are millions of beings in the universe that are part of incarnation program seeking a spirit within a physical existence. They seek to learn as they experience the incarnated life and bringing their newfound knowledge and experiences back to their home worlds and points of existence.

The spirit within soul when it incarnates into the selected physical beings form goes through various stages of transition. The spirit within is always connected to the higher self, all your souls origins vary but the connection process is the same. The souls original form can be a conscious light being to a highly ascended physical being, this is the higher self of the soul. The spirit within is a reflection of a being that has chosen to incarnate into a physical being to help with the ascension of the chosen planet. We call this reflection of self this is described as spirit ethereal multidimensional energy, the spirit within – your soul.

In the moment of incarnation, the ordained transition to the chosen physical beings foetus, the spirit within is a lighter energy set in a frequency for the young earthling in the womb to except – the connection for the Earth life is made. The Earth child is in the heavier 3D energy matrix and the spirit within is from a lighter higher frequencies such as the 5D matrix or beyond. Because of this the vibration frequencies slow blending process is vital for the smooth transition of the soul and this can vary of individual species.

On the day this young being is born is the spirit within second transition. When the youngling takes its first breath the spirit within strengthens into a higher frequency to start the journey of the physical life. Think of your spirit within as a vessel suspended in a multidimensional energy field waiting to slowly release its self to full strength.

As the youngling form develops and grows mentally and physically on its life's journey, so does the soul. The soul always has the knowledge for the young beings journey as this comes from the higher self source. Imagine a silver thread that acts as phone line, always connected so the soul so it can dial home. This silver threat also is the channel for the higher self to monitor its reflection of self – which is the spirit within soul.

There is a point in every beings life journey when the balance of spirit within frequencies and physical body will occur. Now this will vary for each being and species – have you ever heard a human who for example who is 60 years old say "But I feel like I am 32 years old inside". This inner feeling you will have of how old you feel within is the time the soul fully blended and will stay at the set frequencies to death. This will vary for every physical being chosen for incarnation, depending on your purpose of life mission.

While the spirit within is with the chosen physical form it is the Sat Nav for the physical journey. All spirit within souls come with the frequencies to connect to the beings higher consciousnesses to help guide them in their life's and this is known as intuition. All spirit within have a purpose for each individual life and most physical forms will have the sixth sense to connect with their souls true form and their guides. When a being succeeds at this connection great things can occur for the spiritual journey. Have you heard of 'Soul Connection'? – This is vital for the physical being incarnated into, to find its true self and purpose and is a challenge for example in the Earth's 3D energy. The challenge is for the human consciousness to have an open clarity of awareness to connect to the spirit within to trigger it life's purpose. So the human form has to swim out of the heavy 3D energy towards the 5D higher frequencies energy and make a mid-way connection for this to happen. Many lessons will be learned from the individuals life's process of trying to achieve this. If you feel you have not connected to your spirit within soul then this soul work is vital for you to do. This connection to spirit within is the next transition but not many humans achieve this and it is vital to the human ascension process. This is the missing link.

As the human form nears the end of its life the spirit within starts to prepare for its final transition to return home to its home source. The higher self source and guides wait for the spirit within's release from the human form and Earth energies. When this transition occurs the soul travels escorted back to home source blending back with its final form that can be physical or a transitional multidimensional being. Then the final transition is nearly complete.

Depending on the spirit within's life on Earth it might need healing before it leaves the Earths plane and has healing as it reconnects to its higher self. When this is complete it is the final transition of the spirit within for the incarnation process.

We hope this explanation in your Earth language helps you in some way understand the soul spirit within transition processes. Remember a true connection with your spirit within will help you Sat Nav your life and find your true path and self.

We wanted to tell you my story from our point of view in a language you would all understand. The first chapter is the foundation for the rest of the book, helping you to understand the *spirit within* journey in the physical body form of choice. This book will give you the understanding of the various realities and other high ascension beings. It will also bring you wisdom and knowledge for humanity to learn from. We now ask you to sit back and enjoy this experience, as we know it will bring you greater clarity to help you on your life's path while here on earth.

"I am a spiritual being experiencing a physical incarnated life on Earth. I walk in human form, taking human steps and experiencing the third dimension physical plane, learning and collecting knowledge and wisdom on the way. I am happy and at peace with my temporary form. Love and blessings to all."

Aydenline

Chapter 1

Hello, beautiful Earth!

I am brimming over with excitement as I begin this new adventure with you, which I will start by saying, *"Hello, human world!"* Your Mother Earth is a living entity with a beautiful vibration that has shone out into the universe for a very long time. The brilliant world I see is full of rainbow colours, a place of diversity and beauty, and it is a breath of fresh air in the universe where there is so much beauty to behold. Mother Earth is a jewel amongst the stars, and she sings her song out to us as we watch you all from afar.

I would like to introduce myself. My name is Ayderline, and I am a being from a five dimensional planet. I have been chosen to tell you my story of a pure ascended physical being that has made the choice to experience incarnation with physical beings in lower energies and become the spirit within. My hardest task of this chosen role is how to translate it into words in your third dimension Earth language and way of understanding. I will explain to you about my existence and my feelings in a way that helps you understand our existence, the places I have visited, and why we do what we do.

I will take you on a journey that will fire your imaginations, and to points in time you can only ever imagine, writing from my point of view as the spirit within. Each incarnated physical life will be briefly described; giving you a hint of the time frame the person lived in, their character and what I aimed to learn from them on their life's path. Then I will give a breakdown of what I learnt and my reflections back to my world. As I write this, I am the spirit within Sharon living in 2017, and the lives I reveal are some of my past lives which we have allowed her to experience through past life regression for her spiritual development while on Earth. Her past lives are some of the physical life experiences I have undertaken on my spiritual learning path. WOW! Is it not quite amazing, the thought of past lives and the stories we will all have to tell when we return home to our home worlds of existence.

So what is the spirit within? I am a physical energy being capable of multidimensional energy form, a living being with highly ascended telepathic mind powers, and I exist in our world a high frequency energy plane of unconditional love and light. The soul spirit within exists out of time and space in what I can best describe as the NOW moment and is an energy reflection of my true self physical form. Many humans understand that the soul travels home to the spirit realm or heaven. As we said earlier, the souls come from many sources from the universe. I do have a physical planet of existence, but have ascended into the fifth dimensional existence. This allows us to create an ethereal multidimensional split creating the reflection of self, which to you is a soul, the spirit within.

I need to start by explaining the energy of our universe and how it affects the spirit within energy and the Earth in different ways. This involves the physical make up of the universe and the energy of thought.

Every frequency level of energy in the third, fourth and fifth dimensions and beyond, has its own reality, to which a multidimensional form can adapt. As you move through the different levels, your consciousness adapts and raises its frequency to that reality.

Humanity lives in the third dimension **physical lower frequency energy dimension,** known as third dimension physical self. Also within the third dimension is what we call a third dimension matrix, the aim of which is to hold the spirit within in place, and controls the human and spirit within connection while joined on Earth. This means the human will not remember the spirit within previous existences and memories. The challenge has been for spirit within to be the student, learning and full filing a Earth mission. While doing this they try to bring more love and light to your world. Their aim is to trigger in the human a better way of living and existence without the human having prior knowledge to this.

At the moment this is a busy, chattering dimension full of fear, anger and feelings of powerlessness, and you feel lost in the world you live in. You feel you want to do more for your world, but you are swimming against a heavy current, living in hope the tide will change.

There are those who live in the 'Power over Others' group, controlling and manipulating humanity, and then there are the victims, accepting this way of existing. Humans need to stop wanting to be victims, then the behaviour of the controlling power over others will end and aid the ascension process. Humans need to learn to accept that they deserve love; many humans who feel they are victims have an inner belief that they don't deserve love.

In this dimension, you can create your reality through your own mind restrictions – hate attracting hate, love attracting love, a circle of events that keeps repeating the same pattern unless you can see the light of a higher existence. You change your reality by moving your attention to other things – your reality is where your mind is in that moment of your time. For example, you could watch the news and see the biggest massacre shooting in the USA. When you see this kind of event, you are connecting with the fear, anger and confusion of your world and you stay in that spiral of feelings. If you turn your attention to a walk in a beautiful forest and the love you have for your family, you experience kindness, love and peace instead of fear. Do you understand my meaning? If you change your reality as you see it, this will raise your energy. You attract more of the reality your attention is focused on, hate-to-hate, or love-to-love. These also affect your physical body and the powers to self-heal and ascend, keeping you in the time and space of the third dimension reality. But we realised around the time of the Second World War that it is time to break you out of this matrix frame, and to let the spirit within and ascended beings make themselves known to chosen Earth beings. These are Earth beings that have been chosen to be advocates of the ascension beings, to bring forth their healing messages to help humanity. They will remember why they are a spirit within and raise their frequency to help them fulfil their objectives on for example Earth.

We feel the third dimension has now served its purpose, with humanity coming to the point in your time line where you can lift yourselves out of it. To be blunt, if you do not do this, you will destroy yourselves and Mother Earth. Mother Earth is a living entity that has evolved to a higher frequency state of consciousness; she has been helped by us, but the human beings are still in the third dimension frequency and cannot see this change. The animal, mineral and elemental kingdoms are adapting to her new energies that continue to rise. The human mind on its own is not enough for you to ascend; humanity needs to connect with Mother Earth and receive the needed communications from her. When this happens human behaviour will change; by this, we mean how humanity treats Mother Earth. For instance, humans would not treat their best friends the way they treat Mother Earth, with no respect for their welfare – you know in your hearts this is true. When a human succeeds in doing this, they recognise there is something more than just themselves. Now, we know a lot of humans who are light workers and have made this breakthrough, and we recommend meditation as a starting point on this journey to achieve this connection.

The fourth energy dimension we call the fourth dimension astral self. This is what I call the middle ground, and the stepping-stone to the fifth dimension. The fourth dimension is an astral plane that is smoother-flowing, offering possibility and capability, with more clarity of the universe and with that, more hope for humanity. You will find this astral plane while in your dreams and meditation state of being. Have you heard of astral travel while in your dream state? You will find we use this fourth dimension conscious state of being to give you guidance and messages. Because of the rigid 3D energy, many of you will forget about these on awakening, or just after, so it is key to record any unusual dreams. For those of you that have started to raise your vibration, you will remember more of the dreams and visualisations in meditation, but you should still record these as over time, they could fade.

This fourth dimension astral energy plane leads you away from the hate and anger energy towards the love energy, which prepares you for the fifth dimension unconditional love energy. To enter the fourth dimension astral plane you need to raise your state of consciousness by working in the thoughts of peace, kindness, love and light. Some of you are starting to work in this energy dimension with the shift since your year 2000. Since around 2012, this shift has accelerated and there are notable changes in humanity, with its attitude moving more towards the spiritual. The more of you that lift your vibration, the more of you will be transported to the fourth dimension way of thinking and behavior. Your attention will shift to the thinking pattern needed to ascend into the fifth dimension reality and with this, your Earth will become more enlightened and the shift will really begin to move along at a fast pace.

The fifth high frequency energy dimension is a high frequency energy plane that exists in a permanent state of peace, bliss, love, kindness and joy. We like to think of this version of you as the light body self. We have no time or space restraints, we exist in the here and now in unity, with no worries of past or future. No more negative thoughts stream into the mind of a being who has reached fifth dimension consciousness. Your mind is quieter, allowing for telepathic skills and conscious growth; you will be without the constant chatter that flows into the third dimension mind. While in this wonderful fifth dimension, you can also connect to the universe knowledge pot and so much more. You've probably guessed by now in which dimension level I exist. Humanity can exist at this level on Earth, in your human form, if you lose your layers of doubt, anger and fear. There is a lot of information in your Earth's knowledge about this subject, which will fascinate you.

The veil is being lifted off Mother Earth so you can shift into the higher dimensions, which is what many of you tuned into the higher dimensions are now feeling. We are very busy working behind the scenes to help take humanity into this level of ascension. When we say a shift is occurring, the layers between the dimensional realms are very thin at the moment, and this allows us to channel fifth dimension energy to your third dimension level to help you along. The middle platform, the fourth dimension, is there to help you take the next leap of faith and TRUST in your ascension.

Many ascension beings have monitored Mother Earth for millions of your years. It was around 300,000 years ago that earth was a base for creation of more enhanced human life forms and used for the incarnation programme. *(Read* The light within Atlantis *and* New Earth – the light beyond the horizon *for more information on the subject).*

The incarnated spirit within soul and higher self seeks opportunities for the being they have connected with to recognise the love and light of the spirit within, waiting for them to connect mind to spirit and ask for guidance and help. We respect the free will of humanity and other physical beings in the Universe, which is why we mostly wait for you to ask for our assistance. But we do gently nudge you on your life's paths, to help us fulfil what we have come here to learn; we also lay signs on your paths for you to recognise from us. This can be hard due to the human EGO and free will; because of this these are not always seen by you, understood and acted upon, as we would hope. We do understand that how you respond to the spirit within you depends on the part of the world you live in and where you are on your life's journey.

We find it interesting, as the early response of humanity to the spirit within triggered the religions you know today. The divine spark of the unknown was recognised by ancient man, which developed worship amongst humans. It is quite fascinating to us, my friends, how many religions and belief systems have started from the same divine spark of love and how humanity interpreted these signs.

Through our connection with you we also wish to inspire the values of humanity, the core values you live by day-to-day, which need to inspire you into an honest, kind and loving existence. You will find your core values are affected by family, work, religion and belief systems and these base core principle values will guide how you live, and how you behave. If you live in a world of greed and selfishness, for example, and then see the divine light which leads to enlightenment, the contrast will bring you to the 'WE' way of thinking, enabling you to discard the selfish side of your nature. You would have greater understanding of us, which would then lead to your old core values changing, and bringing in a more honest and loving way of being. I hope you understand this! Please reflect on what your core values are, my friends; it's important they are true to you, your heart, and can connect to your core and the spirit within with love and light.

I would like to explain about our two different realities – the ascension beings and Mother Earth – so you can understand the difference between us. I feel the starting point is how we think. We think as one, with the 'WE' in unity, while humans on Earth think as

'I', in isolation from your fellow humans. We are all energy, but within the universe the pure love energy from which we are all formed can take on different ways of existence. For example, your molecules are made up of energy, matter is energy, the space they are created in is energy, and all these form the physical existence you know. I am energy formed from the same source as you, my friends – the divine spark. We are free flowing physical energy with mind, with telepathic thought that creates what we know and see in the fifth dimension energy of unconditional love, living in the NOW.

The beings that choose to incarnate exist in the energy of **unconditional love** and an Earth human exists in the restricted lower frequency energy where the love energy can be lost through fear and anger.

To be honest, I do struggle with the limits of the third dimension language of words to compare us. You will have to use your imaginations and create images of us in your reality, and we are happy for you to see us in the way you interpret us on Earth. For example, I have shown myself as Ayderline in a physical female human form, so you can relate to me in your third dimension energy reality. I do not mean to be patronising, but this is the only way you can understand me at this point in your Earth's time line. If, for example, you had ascended to the fifth dimension energy level, I would reveal myself as I truly am, and you would have no fear and a great understanding, acceptance and clarity of mind to see us as we are. If Earth transcended into the fifth dimensional way of being, you would not have incarnated souls to guide you. You would become the teachers of the universe and join the universal incarnation programme to help others.

As you already understand, I come from a fifth dimensional planet and you come from three dimensional Mother Earth. My friends, your world is a beautiful place as we see it, but over the last two hundred years we have sadly watched you pollute your world due to humanities growth in population, technology and greed. It is now getting to the point where it will be hard for Mother Earth to heal herself, but there is still opportunity to help her. Just take a step back and look at the comparisons I make of our two worlds in these next few paragraphs, and this will inspire you to look at your planet in a new light. I do have to add at this point that I cannot blame you alone; you have had off-world influences in your technology, which have advanced your societies too quickly. We know you did not have the chance to ascend as needed with this advancement, and it's almost as if it's all got out of control for you and caused an imbalance in societies across your world. You have wealthy countries advancing in their technologies leaving your under developed countries behind, but our dream is for humanity to be balanced more equally for your future survival.

While I have been on your Earth I have greatly admired your nature, your mountains, even your volcanoes because of the strength and energy they possess. I have witnessed beautiful spaces on Earth that take my breath away. Some of these include the oceans and waterways, which vary so much and are a must for all to see, from the iced rivers to the clear tropical seas. I am also aware of the climate with your winds, rain, sun and the seasons created for your planet as it rotates around the sun and the moon rotates around the earth. It is quite an exceptional place, my friends; you are all so lucky to have such a beautiful planet.

I have been fascinated by all the different plant and animal species in your world. Your environment was well balanced up to about one hundred and fifty years ago, when man started to invade the lands more. Wildlife naturally kept itself to controllable numbers depending on their habitats, but these are being taken from them and causing the imbalance within nature and the animal kingdom. You might think it's sad when animals kill other animals, but when a world creates millions of animals and creatures, there will always be a hierarchy of supremacy and the fittest survives, as this is the law of the Earth's animal kingdom. You would naturally get one or two animal extinctions due to nature, but humanity is extinguishing Mother Earth's wildlife through pollution and the mismanagement of your world. When you reach the fifth dimension ascension, your animal kingdom will be managed by humanity for the best of the animals, not humanity. You will find they will return to their natural way of being as they do not have the intelligence or the DNA make-up to ascend as you can, but they can be as they should be, living safely alongside humanity.

I have also witnessed the cruelty of nature on Earth, for example how the sea can claim boats, lands and lives. But remember this is all part of your world and surviving her; she is a formidable living energy, but she also has great love, healing and power for you all. Remember, my friends, your Mother Earth is a living being, she is a planet that is trying to survive as well. You will find the more humanity pollutes her, the more she loses the struggle of survival. At the moment, Mother Earth is wounded and she will fight back, trying to rebalance her world. You are experiencing her fighting back with more severe weather patterns battering beautiful parts of your world as she tries to rebalance. We see so much more than you can, we see the spirit within her, also the elemental beings veiled from you, and believe me, they are struggling to keep Earth balanced. So please, as you read these words, make yourself aware of this and help them. I'm sorry if I have shocked you with my forthright words so early on but I care so much for Earth's people and I had to take this opportunity to speak to you about it.

As you know, your world is made of different continents and different races with fascinating cultures, all with family units. It has been with great interest that we have watched the lands divide and humanity spread across your world. In your ancient times, we witnessed off-world beings creating their homes on Earth too, which led to them leaving their influence in your DNA. The evidence of their existence is carved in caves and recorded in words; evidence yet to be found by you also lies deep in the oceans and under the ice. Take time to explore your books and Internet for all the evidence that is available for you to learn from today. I also know the day of disclosure to you from your governments, the people with the power over you, is not that far away and the more your voices are heard the sooner this will happen for you, so that humanity can make its own judgements together as one, and start ascending.

I would like to add a plug for Mother Earth here - When you next use a plastic bottle, think of all the rubbish in your waterways across your planet, think about what humanity is doing to this beautiful world of yours, slowly choking her with man's waste. As I am still here on Earth with an Earth being, I witness the news. Most recently as I write this, your great barrier reefs are dying and the beauty your Mother Earth, once beheld, is disappearing. I remember a time when the world population was smaller and Earth was unpolluted. Can you imagine the beauty your Mother Earth held then my friends? It was as you say, 'an awesome sight to see', and you can create that again if you act now.

The beauty on Mother Earth is unique, a beauty in itself not seen anywhere else, while the beauty of what exists in my world is not what you will ever see on Earth. You all come from various places in the universe, and deep within you all is a memory of your home existence. Some of you have learnt to tap into this by meditation and past life regressions. Soul connection is key to this link with your home source and your inner soul connection. When you have achieved this, we only show you a glimpse of what you will come home to, as the love and energy is so powerful, it would blow your human mind while in the restricted third dimension energy plane. When you have experienced this and you draw back from this pure love energy, some of you will experience emotion and feel loss, as you recognise what you do not have on the Earth plane.

The universe is over seen by the overseers, this is a life force; that seek out beings that wish to work in the love and the light existence. They have sixty-five ascension levels in these dimensional realms of existence. God, as Earth humans call our overseers, sits in the sixty-fifth level with the highest ascended archangels and other highly ascended ascension beings from other planets, realms and dimensions. As we ascend in on our spiritual journey, we learn from the other ascended beings how to gain the knowledge we need to progress and develop. In the lower ascension levels, we are all telepathic with a great knowledge of the universe. Each time we ascend, our conscious energy expands and becomes more powerful with each ascension stage. With this newfound power comes a great knowing of what lies beyond the dimensions. By the time we reach the level of Archangel ascension, we would have vast awareness of the entire universe, and the high-ascended beings all work as a collective for the good of all.

I also want to explain that the overseers levels, has inner dimensional realms all linking to the ascension levels. One of these inner realms is the nature and animal realm, which you also call the nature and animal kingdom, and many of you use the symbolism of the rainbow bridge as a link, taking your animals and pets back to this realm.

All creatures on Earth have a spirit within and all come back to the nature and animal realm, where they continue to grow and develop their energies. You often ask if your pets link up with you when you come back home and yes, my friends, they do. They have been part of your journey and learning and they will always have a bond with the spirit within through the physical lives you shared.

There is also an Elemental realm, many of you will have heard of the Elemental beings on Earth, which are vital to your Earth's existence; they cleanse, purify and help protect Mother Earth. The fairies, elves, tree spirits, mermaids, dragons and unicorns are just a few of the Elemental beings living in one of the energy planes in your Earth's energy fields. A lot of humanity will be unaware of this, as they are of the spirit realm, but their existence is real, my friends. Elemental beings were on the Earth plane in a third-fourth dimension existence when they lived among man many, many centuries ago, but they raised themselves up into a higher plane of energy – the metaphysical level. To picture this, imagine that they pulled a magical cloak over themselves as protection against humanity's naivety and fear about any beings different to themselves.

Your Earth has what we call energy planes – they are not realms or dimensions – which run alongside your existence; imagine that as you walk through the air you breathe, you walk through their world too. We hope this makes sense to you, my friends, because trying to explain the different layers of existence around Earth is hard, as there are not many Earth words that can help me with this. The elementals that lived amongst you thousands of years ago had to make this decision, as other forces came to Earth and humanities limited thinking could not accept them, as they were so different. Some of this rejection was made through ignorance – not understanding the good they could do, or the magic they could bring to Earth. I have witnessed this many times while on the Earth plane; the persecution of people or societies that don't fit into certain people's way of thinking, or the feeling that what they don't understand becomes a threat to their way of life.

The Elementals are like you – they have spirit within and return home to the elemental realm. Their realm is a beautiful fairyland that sparkles and sings, and you will hear jingling, playful laughter and soft music as you pass through. They have a pure, loving existence with the purpose of looking after the nature and animal realm of our world, as they do on your Earth. Any being from any level can visit this realm, linking with their energies and old friends. To take this to the next step for you they visit other realms, worlds and dimensions too. Elementals have been known to choose to take on a physical Earth form existence, as we do, so they can carry out a specific purpose on Earth. Do you know any humans that are very petite, with angelic or pixie features, or redheads with passion, or great swimmers who love the water and are keen to look after the environment? These are most likely elementals, reincarnated to help the Earth at this time.

We have such contrast in our different realities, and I hope this simple description helps you understand the difference, as there are vast differences that exist between the other worlds, realms and dimensions we visit. We have encountered other beings that have great love or have high respect for each other, and some of these have reached high ascension levels, but we know none of them will reach our highest pure divine state of ascension. But this is of no consequence, because our teachings to these other beings are to bring in love and light and a better of way of existence. For us to witness any ascension amongst the universe is wonderful for us, as it helps to bring the universe together in love and light.

Mother Earth has had thousands of years to develop into what you now know and in the last 150 years, humanity has spread and populated the world, causing wars and frictions within your civilisations. Sadly for humanity, we also see that the restricted third dimension view of survival has hurt nature mainly through ignorance as well as for economic reasons. Humans are struggling to step out of the third dimension restrictions and into the fourth dimension ascended level, trying to make humanity more open to the process of acceptance – many people will not step away from the damage they are doing, because of greed and the fear of the unknown. But please realise it's not too late and you can limit further damage and try correct the mistakes of the last 150 years or more. Your technology can now bring clean energy for all, if only the humans with powers over your Earth would let you ascend to live like this.

Please go out and take a look at your world, my friends, be more caring and more observant. It's not just your own mind-set changing to bring in the love and the light; it's also how you respect your Mother Earth and others within it. I have had conversations with my ascension friends, and we feel we want to ascend to Earth, shake you all up and march your streets, giving out this message to you all. But we know in reality that as you are at the moment, humanity would not cope with the shock of our alien spirit existence. So we are trying to make you all aware in a discreet way, slowly bringing more love and light to humanity, through people and words. We are getting a little concerned as we realise we need this process to accelerate, so we are going to speed things up. More star children will be born to be healers, teachers and mediums to spread the word. Through an awakening spirituality will spread across the lands over the next 50 years, people will question their existence and the way they live, and you will ascend into the fourth dimension way of being. This will prepare life on Earth for the final ascension of acceptance of other beings from other worlds, and access the universal knowledge pot of knowledge, with all living in a loving, pure love and light way of being.

I know I digressed again, but my passion for healing Earth is so strong that as we compare our two realities, the one thing that really stands out to me is the difference in the way we treat each other – and this is the key to your ascension. Remember, I have lived a few lives on Earth – the first one was in 403AD and I am still here in 2017! I have seen so many changes on Earth each time I have visited, and I also have access to the knowledge of your time lines, which show me a mixture of dark and light existences without much ascension progress. I have learnt to not let these past existences and events dwell within my core, I just have to know that as the spirit within, I am doing everything I can to help your world, and these words are part of this process. As well as learning and ascending in the spirit realm, with every physical existence I experience, I aim to help that being to be the best they can to help the world they live in, and to spread the love and the light to all.

I work with my incarnation team, (on Earth, you call them soul groups) made up of a few light beings, and everyone is a unique individual. I have been part of the same soul based program family from my start of this incarnation journey, and they support and guide me through my ascension levels of learning. We are all at various levels, all ascending at different times, but we stay together linked by our minds, similar to what you would know on Earth as a family bond.

Being part of incarnation program come with an ethos of guidance set out by the overseers. These create my core values. The simple basis of our true core values for your understanding is below:

- Giving unconditional love to all through our actions, thoughts and presence
- Living in the unity of 'WE' as a collective while maintaining the individual
- Treating each other with the highest regard
- Bringing pure love and light to all intelligent beings in the universe
- All thoughts and actions are for the best outcome for all involved
- Our teachings are true and pure for all
- Guiding others to find their true self and values
- Experiencing the knowledge to create the wisdom for learning and guidance.

I am a recognised healer on my planet my teachings were adjusted so my development and understanding could learn, part of which involved observing other healers at work with other beings that returned from a physical incarnation existence. I also studied in 'The great halls of learning', where all knowledge and events to do with healing practices in our world are stored. I was guided to the knowledge I would need, but as with any role, you don't truly know the job until you start to practice it. This was a gradual process for me, and eventually I was allowed to assist another healer and help cleanse the spirit within energies when they came back from their physical incarnated existences. Then the moment came when I was allowed to oversee the first healing process on my own. You can see, my friends, that we are educated and developed as you would be, just like an Earth nurse or doctor – when they are qualified, they can practice unsupervised on their own, under an umbrella of higher authority.

My role as a healer is so interesting; I help beings and their spirit within that come home to us from a physical incarnation existence, as you would understand it on other worlds, realms and dimensions. I help them look at the physical life they have led and remove any negative energy they have brought back with them. Quite often these chosen lives are not in the high-energy plane, but in a lower energy such as Earth's. Before my friends have gone to their chosen physical existence, I have sat with them and their incarnation team here in our world, and helped them plan a map of their journey on their incarnated life's path. This plan should benefit their ascension and benefit the place they are visiting. I am involved at this stage so I have an understanding of what they are trying to learn so we can compare this to the life they led and what they learnt while in that incarnated physical existence. This is a job as you would describe it but I don't have the time restraints you have on Earth and some of the other physical worlds we visit. I have ascended masters that teach and guide me and I suppose from your point of view I answer to them, as they aid in my learning. In between all this learning, which is something we all love to do, we also play, meet up, talk, listen to music, follow our passions – one of mine is botanical plants of different worlds. I have a collection from various worlds, stored in a reality created by me, where I can visit, observe and learn about the plants I collect.

There are a few reasons we have the healing I mentioned. One of them concerns the time when I started to absorb the knowledge in 'The great halls of learning', where other healers record what they have seen when helping other beings that have come back from a incarnated physical existence. These experiences touch us in ways we are not used to, because some of them involve the pain and fears a physical being has felt, as we need to face all that is experienced.

Because we do not know pain or fear in our world, these emotions can affect our energies, as we are very sensitive and have only pure love energy feelings. We keep ourselves healed for this reason, my friends, so we stay cleansed and pure as we can. I had to learn not to take on the worries of other existences, and my conscious energy mind is formed in such a way that I can cope with this. I can care and send love and healing to these places, but it does not prevent me being who I am and working at the highest and best I can for the good of all.

My incarnation team contains many levels of ascension beings. Those that choose not to take on a incarnation physical existence will absorb all the knowledge that comes back into our team to learn from. As they ascend and mature, a bit like reaching adulthood in your world, they will be guided to make their own decisions and take their own path in my world. We do have different roles; I am a healer, a few other roles we have are teachers, organisers, explorers, scientists and philosophers.

The archangels are pure love and light beings who have not touched a incarnated physical plane existence and they stay highly ascended in the upper levels with the overseers. At any point in time, through thought, they can be with thousands of spirit within that are on a incarnated physical life journey. Also remember that physical beings can call upon them for their help, which is only a thought away; the archangels have great knowledge, healing powers and wisdom, and their individual powers are beyond anything you could ever imagine. As an observer of physical civilisations, it is also of interest to me how each one portrays these divine beings of pure unconditional love. The artist on Earth, for instance, portrays them with wings, which is understandable because of how they have shown themselves to chosen Earth beings. Some archangels have chosen to show themselves in human form and the energy that is around and behind them looks like wings; so when the stories have been told, the human artist's eye interprets what they heard and expressed it as wings of flight in their art and words.

Once I decided my journey was to be as a healer in my world, I knew where I was going in my life and understood my existence. I looked at the various options with my teachers and mentors, and one of the things I wanted to be as part of my healing role was a guide to other beings that are experiencing a incarnated physical existence. In our world, we believe that to truly understand what another feels and experiences and to be able to guide them, you need to experience that physical existence yourself.

It was decided a long, long time ago that when we incarnate with the physical being energy forms, the spirit within would not be able to pass to the physical bodies mind the memories of the higher self home world, unless we choose to. The only reason we would have done this is for the benefit of their spiritual development and the ascension of that being. We created an invisible veil, which is hidden from you, behind which the spirit within the physical body can exist, staying all-knowing and able to see and understand what is happening in the home worlds and on the chosen incarnation physical existence we spoke of earlier. From our incarnation team we are monitored, protected and healed as needed while on this incarnated physical life's path. A percentage of our spirit comes to the baby being when developing in the womb, and as this being grows and develops, more and more of our projected spirit will filter to the physical body. Eventually, there comes the point of maturity of the physical being form and the spirit within, which happens when the balance is correct, and we maintain that balance for the rest of that physical existence.

When I was talking about the reason we connect with physical forms for incarnation, I should have mentioned that one of the main reasons we connect with physical beings is the desire to bring love and light into their world. So part of my path would be to have ensured they have lived in the best way they can. But as you are aware, all physical energy beings have self-will and most have egos too, so it can be hard for us to achieve this, my friends. If lessons have not been learned by the time we return to our home existences, we can choose to go back to another incarnated physical energy being life to try and learn these lessons again, or we might choose to move on and look for new teachings and experiences.

When I go to what we have asked you to call 'The great halls of learning', this is a space where we can study and learn all that has gone before, and possible future time lines are also stored in this massive knowledge pot. We do not have – and do not need – computers and an Internet that stores information like you do in your world. We can access this knowledge with a thought; our thoughts are our trigger, like the computer mouse, that guides us to where we need to be in the area of learning. When I studied healing and how other guides have helped spirit within (souls) that travel to a physical plane to keep them safe and healed, I also learned about when they return home and how the healers worked with them. I have guidance from my teachers and mentors of where to look in the time lines of knowledge for what would be beneficial to me in my studies. So with a thought, I can look at moments in the past; we see it as you would see a film on a film reel, seeing moments of that reality.

As we have said, we do not have time as you understand it, but we do understand the concept of time and we can glimpse into the past on your time frame for the right information. The wonderful thing about this is that we can look at all perspectives of the situation we are over-viewing, including how the physical being felt, how others felt around them, and how this affected them all. We can also study how the spirit within was feeling and their awareness of the situation, and then we can look at how the higher self, back in their home world dealt with this experience. I suppose the nearest you might understand this experience on Earth is for those of you who are capable of 'Remote Viewing'. This involves your mind going into the past, seeing a past event taking place and experiencing any feelings from that moment in time. You are connecting to a recording of energy that will always be there, as well as the energy of the person you are seeking. Energy beings' life prints remain in the Earth's energy fields for you to connect with; it is your thought and intent that allows you this connection.

I can also use this same method of looking into the past for glimpses of the future. For example, for every physical life I have chosen to take, we have looked into the future of that life using remote viewing. We see periods of that life where I can learn what I wish to learn, based on a life's path that has been previously set. Remember, that most human beings is not aware of this planned life path, but the spirit within and their higher self is aware, as are their guides and incarnation team, which holds the blue-prints of this plan. But we would like to say that futures are not set and can be altered with your thoughts.

My team, as I call them, guides me while on this physical life journey, and when I come back home we have the healing process. After the physical existence, we use the same technique again to go back into time and study situations that need healing. We choose not to look at the whole future of humanity because at the moment, we are trying to steer you all to love, light and ascension. This is because we know this is achievable, but as you stand at the moment, in the negative third dimension energy, we could look two years or 50 years ahead and not see a change in humanity's future. This is because as you are at the moment, this would not be achievable without humanity changing for the better. But as we progress with you all and the Earth energies alter, and the vibration is raised more into love and light, we could look again, in a few months or years, to 50 years ahead, and see a different future. So you see, my friends, the futures are set based on where you are now, so you can change your future, you can alter your lives and Earth's future existence for the better. It's very interesting, my friends, as you can imagine, what we can achieve; we have overseers that are always accessing the future, as this helps us see how our work on Earth is progressing. This also allows us to access you, and helps us decide what we have to do for humanity to be the highest and best they can be.

For my first physical energy life form, I chose Mother Earth. Mother Earth has been one of the most popular destinations for our ascension learning, as it is such a diverse planet, with humanity's unique characteristics and off-world alien influences. I chose the time of 403AD, when the world was in some disarray, as nations grew and battled for supremacy over each other, a time of challenge for us to bring love and light to your world. Yes, there were hardships on Earth, there were wars, but it was also a simpler existence for humanity, learning to survive in day-to-day life.

The planning was complete, we had mapped out my life's path, and this was a very exciting time for me as we set the moment to go into the physical form. I gathered with my incarnation team, the chosen healers and the guides that would support me on this journey, and on my return to my home world. Part of the planning process was to look at what I wanted to learn from this physical life, and we picked a family that would fulfil this. I wanted to experience conflict of emotions, to know what it felt like when your heart wants to do one thing but you have to do another because of life's circumstances. I also wanted to experience the love of a parent and to be a parent, and alongside this, hard work, compassion and wealth. Wealth of money is something we do not have in our world; you could say we have wealth in other ways in abundance, as we have love, light, kindness, support and compassion. This is true wealth, my friends, not the materialistic things you experience while on Earth. I chose to be born into a wealthy family, not for my own gratification or comfort, but just to experience this, as there are sometimes hardships that come with having financial wealth in life.

I wish to explain here about the guides that supported me on my journey while I was on the incarnation experience. At least three guides join the chosen being that is to connect with the physical form. One of these guides will be with you throughout your whole physical life and is your door to high dimensional realms. You sometimes know this main guide as your Gate Keeper; their purpose is to offer guidance and protection to you on your incarnated life's path. Other guides will leave and join you through your life's path, as you reach different stages where you need extra support for example, education, relationships, parenthood, illness and your spiritual path. Your guides are made up of a combination of angels, high ascension beings and elemental/animals guides. Some of the guides would have had a physical experience of Earth. We plan and work together to help my journey as the spirit within, to bring the love, light and wisdom to the physical being and their world.

I always wondered what it would be like to connect with a physical form and I imagine you do too. It's not like your film 'The Body Snatchers', where aliens enter the body, take over the human mind and control them – remember, we let you have a certain amount of free will. We do it by thought energy light, colour and harmonic sound. We use our thoughts to guide the reflection of self to joining the spirit within to the chosen physical form. Our joint thoughts help create the chosen reflection of self to form the energy state they need to be in to make the transformation and project themselves into the chosen physical being. As you can imagine, we have lots of different thoughts all the time, so this process has to be done in a very controlled and serious way, ensuring our thoughts only focus on the task in hand. In common with other beings on planets, realms and dimensions, the energies of the chosen physical beings all vary, and we have to learn the energy frequency and vibrations of their existence. This energy varies for every human, as well as the area of the world and timeline we are going into. We have centuries of experience in connecting to the physical form; we have science-based beings working at this who have refined this down to a success rate of 99.9.9%.

One of the things I realised as I joined with a physical being was that I would experience all they sense in life – I would share what they see through their eyes, what they taste, smell, touch and hear, because my spirit is connected to the whole of the being's body. I am joined to the physical form with thin little silver energy threads going to every part of the physical body, like sensor probes that pick up all feelings. It's as if I shut my eyes and live the moments of your time, experiencing everything with this human form – and this is an invisible event for you, my friends. So with every physical being we touch, it is an intimate experience as you can imagine, because there are times when you cry, are ill, have laughter, sexual experiences and we feel and see all of this with you from our first connection. We can visit your Earth, we draw our energies close to you on the Earth plane; we see your health and energy levels and hear your thoughts, but the spirit within feels and experiences so much more, it is quite amazing for us.

At risk of making you laugh, if you believe in us, you must often wonder if we are there watching you all the time – even when you are relieving yourselves on your toilets! Well, I can guarantee that your guides are very discreet, as this does not interest them; we also see your spirit within energy more that your physical form – and we are sensitive to any feelings of discomfort. But the spirit within does go through all this with you, because it's part of the physical experience.

We do try to send you healing when you are ill, but with the human ego, mind, negativity, doubts and low energies, it is sometimes hard for this healing to penetrate your energy field; you need to be open to us to receive this healing. We care all the time for you, but even those of you who wonder why you have had dark times, don't realise this is because your own human essence has blocked us. We are always trying to help, so open your heart to this and help us help you, my friends.

One of the most interesting feelings we come across when we join with a lower physical being, comes from the beings that give love and love each other in a physical way. It is interesting to us how you feel, your sexual urges and pleasures, compared to what we experience. In your world you have individuals you have labelled some homosexual or lesbian and some of humanity are offended by their existence, where two of your beings of the same gender love and care for each other. But you know, my friends, you should embrace this as it's not just to do with the body, it is also to do with the spirit within. Humans are drawn by energy when bonding, like for like from the same incarnation team, and what is key is to find the unconditional love and the comfort you need to be happy in whatever form.

It is lovely to experience the purest love a human can give in whatever form it takes. Of course it's not as I experience it in the my world, but it lightens our hearts when we see the love for a child, wife or partner, the true love I am talking about, the true love when you say I have found my soul mate; that is when you know, my friends. I would suggest if you are not in a relationship of true love, then you are not in the right relationship. If this is the case, you need to re-evaluate your life. (Please do not mind me giving you bits of advice through these words, but this book is to learn from and to make you think about your own life, as well as reading about my spirit within lives with different physical beings).

A reflection of self, spirit within is connected to you from within and are protected from your fears, anger, anxiety and dreads of life; this is because we are cocooned and protected. Ee get a constant flow of healing – and through this, our energies are kept balanced. We are aware of what goes on within you and around you, but we don't let the emotions you feel attach to us. This is because it would affect our pure energies too much and if we allowed all of these emotions and negative energy to affect us, we would not be able to stay in the physical form for the life span decided. So that is why we use the word cocooned a lot, as we are protected in a force field of healing, pure energy within you, but also fully connected to you at the same time.

Chapter 2

Spirit within Alexander - *Earth*

My first physical life experience was to be born into the human form that would be known as Alexander Manouil. When the time came and my reflection of self was blended with this human life, I discovered that while connected to this being, I could see, hear and feel everything that was going on around me. The spirit within this human form was part of my higher self in my existence, staying connected at all times. As you know, this was a new experience, it was all so exciting and wonderful to behold. I was looking forward to my Earth journey with Alexander and as I write my words I'll give you the essence of it from my experience as the spirit within, a glimpse of his human personality and what the time he lived in was like.

So how did I feel when I started my first journey to the physical form? I felt my own energy alter, I felt my energy separate but remain connected to my higher self and incarnation team. My thoughts were as one with my team which was guiding me and we shared the experience as my spirit within went to the chosen Earth being in his mother's womb. This part of me was conscious of my higher self, and it was placed within the living form and cocooned, hidden by our spiritual veil of protection and love. I was aware of everything as the baby finished developing, experiencing its growth and any sensations and feelings, which extended to awareness of the world outside the womb. I waited patiently for when the newborn baby chose to leave the womb to start his life on his Earth path. All of this information was fed back to me, as her higher self from the spirit within. I felt fine, even though a part of my energy was leaving for a period of time to be in the physical form, knowing we would always be connected.

What was also wonderful was that this part of my energy could come out of this physical human body whenever I chose, when the human body was sleeping. My spirit within could link back with me to full energy levels and go and collect further knowledge, but I was always connected, monitoring the human being I was part of, returning before they awoke. We can achieve this because of our vast conscious mind, which has a unique thought process that allows us to function like this, whilst remaining part of a collective of energy and thoughts.

I mentioned leaving the physical body while they slept. In case you were wondering, we are not cocooned for years in the time we spend within the physical body. Have you heard of the term astral travelling in your world, and humans that have had outer body experiences while they have been sleeping? This occurs when my energy form leaves the physical being to join my higher self. I spend time in the fourth dimension astral plane and connect with my fifth dimension energy friends. I feel whole, but the separation does limit our actions, so we make the most of our full strength energies as often as we can. We have this now so well practiced that the human form is unaware of this, unless we choose to let you know for their spiritual path development.

The interesting part of any physical connection is their belief systems and the history behind them. Remember, part of any incarnation journey we take with a physical being is to bring love and light. This is so they will become a better being, bringing light to their world, realm or dimension. Every journey we take on this path is a challenge, some more than others, depending on where the chosen race is in their ascension path. At the time I joined with Alexander, the Greeks were still living under the Roman influence of their religion and beliefs. When the Roman republic conquered Greece in 146BC, they took much of the Greek religion, mythology, culture such as literary and architectural styles, and their gods. The Romans realised the Greeks had a highly advanced civilization, with great philosophers. The Romans worshipped gods, as did the Greeks, so it was natural for them to merge the two belief systems.

The Greeks believed that gods and goddesses watched over them. These gods were like humans but larger in stature; they were immortal and much more powerful than humans, and they felt human emotions like love, anger and jealousy. The Greeks thought the gods lived high above Mount Olympus, in a palace in the clouds, and from there, they kept an eye on life below. Their ancient writings and art show that from time to time they would interfere with what was happening on Earth. They could send storms if they were angry, decide who would be victorious in wars, and sometimes they even played tricks on humans. The Romans believed in gods but their portrayals were not so mythical. They portrayed their gods travelling in chariots to reach above the clouds, and there are many stories of gods, their names and acts on Earth. With the mythical elements coming into this ancient history, humanity has been trying to understand if these were just stories or myths from times gone by, or actual events. Some ask if the gods were aliens, or whether this religion could emanate from a glimpse of the divine spark of love and light, and the people's interpretation of the unknown. Remember, all through your history there are many examples of literature, like your bible, that are full of stories of men and women that have created miracles with the help of gods.

One of the visiting off-world species I would like to tell you about is called Drygonmi, who came to earth in spaceships, giving knowledge and wisdom to humanity. They are smaller than humankind, with a skin that you would think of as having a lizard texture, but with human form – four limbs and a head, just like you. They come from a highly advanced, peaceful world, travelling the universe as explorers. They communicated to you telepathically when they arrived. Their influences can be found in the advancement of the Greek and Roman cultures around 3000-4000 years ago, which spread across your lands and influenced other cultures. Now ask yourselves: where did the Greek and Roman gods come from? In Greek mythology, there are tales of heroes, gods and demigods that walk among mortals, have great powers, great knowledge and are capable of saving or destroying humanity. But these tales go beyond your Greek mythology; all over the world there are amazing tales of heroes and gods and in all of those tales, these mythological creatures are described as having powers beyond human capabilities. They are part of our intergalactic council and we interact with this highly ascended race, some choosing to be guides to humanity; this is no different to what we do from our world.

So you see, from the visit of this alien race, man had to interpret what they did not understand, so behind the myths and gods is a real event in your ancient history – a visit from an alien civilisation. I thought this would be of interest to you as you read these words

When Alexander was created, a percentage of my reflection of self became part of him and as he grew we could slowly filter more of the spirit within to him. There is a future point when the spirit within split between human and spirit is balanced within his human form. When this particular event happens, it varies with all physical forms; it is a gradual process, occurring at a point of human maturity in the physical make-up and mind. This has to be slow process, because if we suddenly blended with a young baby at the full spirit within strength, it would be a shock to both the human body and my pure energy system. Throughout my journey with any physical form, I receive guidance and healing from his guides and my incarnation team as the life progresses.

As to us making you aware of your journey's path, the spirit within knows your life plan; it's the human, their mind and the essence of the human that does not know. As we enter your body, your own human essence – you could call it your human spirit – lives alongside us. If we were not part of your existence and being part of you individually, you would still live your lives, but it would be in a darker, unhappier existence. You would let your egos rule your minds and body; you would have little sense of good, love and kindness without our pure love energy. The question is: How would humanity have developed without us? And we can see the separate time lines that answer this, and what we see is not a nice picture, so we know we are right to bring the love and light into humanity.

With all our connections to the universe, we know that having the spirit within only benefits you for the highest and best outcome. We do not try to control you, as you know you have free will and you make your own choices through your lives. We choose to present you good choices around love and kindness, guiding you away from hate and misery. How you choose is up to you. If you choose the misery, then that is what you will know in your lifetime, as you will give out negative energies and draw the negative energies back in. It might not always be the spirit path you have chosen, my friend, but we let you divert if it's your choice. Having said that, we do try to steer you back to the love and light path as this is our mission. If you still choose misery, then we have to accept this as part of the experience. But remember, what we truly seek is for the human essence to recognise the pure loving and light spirit within you, as we do with all physical experiences we have throughout the universe.

The way I explain this is that humanity creates its own reality; in other words, you are creating what is happening in your world. In your limited third dimension energy at the moment, you restrict yourselves through your fears and misconception of everything, which then draws in the negative way of thinking. But as you change all this and take your attention into the fourth dimension clear way of thinking pattern, humanity will change its perception of each other for the better. You will then find the world's energy will lighten and draw in the love and light energy of the divine. THEN you ascend into the fifth dimension energy plane and oh my, that will be an amazing day for you all. I'll tell you a little secret: I am already planning to come back to Earth to experience these stages with you and help humanity ascend.

Alexander's home on Earth was in Ancient Greece in 403AD in Dyrrhachium, known today in your modern world as Durrës, part of Albania. Since Alexander's time it has had a few name changes, and in your ancient times Dyrrhachium was a seaport on the route between Rome and the East. The ancient name of the city was Epidamnus before the Romans changed it to Dyrrhachium. An earthquake destroyed Dyrrhachium in 314AD, just before the end of the Roman conquest in 324AD; it was rebuilt and flourished as a province of Epirus Nova, and later became part of the Byzantine Empire. The people lived for years under Roman rule and during the Civil Wars in this area it was the headquarters of Pompey, who kept his military stores there in 345AD.

Alexander was the third child, there was also two elder children which were daughters and eventually, there were seven siblings in total, with Alexander being the eldest son. As well as two older sisters, Evgenia and Kallsto, there were two younger sisters, Myeine and Phaidra, and his parents were also blessed with two further sons, Laios and Pausanius. I witnessed the great celebration at Alexander's birth, because to have a son was important for the family business and carrying on the family name. Back in those days, the son was more important than the daughters because they would help bring in the income, and often were the main providers of the families. It was also important to carry on the family name and I still see this in some societies in your modern world today.

He was much loved by two very doting parents, one a loving, nurturing mother Aoede and his father Kleobis, a merchant and very wealthy businessman. Even though he was busy, his father still found time as Alexander grew up to go fishing with him, and take him to his business during the day. I soon realised the trips to his father's work turned out to be his main education as the oldest son. It was important Alexander understood the business, meet the people that worked for his father, and understood the decisions that his father took. The family also had servants, as you would have called them on Earth – not slaves, but people who were employed to serve them. Some helped in the house, others in the business. As a merchant with a fleet of ships, his father had great wealth; he also had a lot of land bringing wealth as well. He was a prominent member of his society and respected by many.

From the view of the spirit within I experienced as a baby, Alexander had quite a protected early life, involving much love and play time. He would run around with his other siblings as they all grew, and it was not until he got to the age of about seven that I noticed things started to change on his life's path. As already said, his father would spend time with him which increased as he got older, and he also started to have education in language and numbers as well as the business. Alexander was a very bright young boy and very curious in his character, which I loved. He absorbed all this learning like a sponge absorbs water – he had what you call a thirst for learning, as I did. With this, I found spirit within and human were working well together, and I loved his enthusiasm for life and everything new. I was intrigued to see and learn how the human mind absorbed knowledge, and learn about the world around them. All of the information comes into the mind through sight, sound, touch, smell and spoken language. Your amazing human brain translates all the information into knowledge, and waits until it's called upon as needed. Humans also have DNA back-up, which gave Alexander the family look and traits that are born within him, while his ego gave him the necessary survival instincts.

Here is a little information about his home. It was within a high walled structure, built on stone foundations; the walls were made of sun-dried mud and stone, and the roofs were lovely red clay tiles. They were a wealthy family, which meant they had a high status house and their home was built around the edge of the walled structure with two inner courtyards. One courtyard was a beautiful garden with a fountain and seating spaces; the other courtyard was the more practical living space, for washing and everyday life. The garden courtyard was a place where the women of the house liked to gather to see and talk as the children played, it was a fun space to be in. They had their own water well too, which was quite a privilege in this hot climate of Greece, as most people had to use communal water sources, collecting it every day for survival. I did observe the odours of the city from human waste and decaying food, which could be very strong at times. This was due to the hot weather, flies and rats – it was hard for the humans to keep the streets clean from waste and decay at this time.

As Alexander was the eldest son, he led the way in setting the example of behaviour and what was expected from a son within the household. The daughters of the house were educated in how to run a house and deal with servants, also learning to sew, cook, and prepare herbal medicines. Their purpose in life in this timeframe was eventually to marry and have their own children. Their parents would wish them to marry into wealthy families and they would bring a dowry to the marriage. Alexander's two elder sisters had marriages arranged at an early stage in their lives, while the two younger sisters met their husbands in the course of their teenage years; as you can imagine, finding husbands for four daughters was a lot to take on in any timeline!

From what I have learnt of the human children, I found Alexander was a typical little boy; he loved hunting animals, swimming, diving for shells and hunting for treasure with his brothers. He also loved games and fishing, and was a real outdoor young man which I loved, as I also loved being in nature. I have to admit that as the spirit within, I really enjoyed this, because I could see more of the world and understand it. One of my favorite things was watching Alexander swim in the crystal clear seas; I loved the blue of the Earth sky reflecting in the water, and nature under the waves. This was so beautiful and a privilege to be part of. When he dived into the cool, clear sea I would feel and see all of it, everything he did; I was there with him, experiencing it as Alexander did.

So as we thought it would be, my role in his younger life with his family was to nurture him and keep him safe and alongside this, experience the love of parents, his siblings and friends. Then the education started which I found very exciting, because if I wished, I could see every single moment that would be on my Earth being's physical pathway. But we choose not to learn this before we go, because part of this Earth experience is for me, as the student within, to learn. I learn about the body I am in and I learn about the feelings that physical beings experience. This is all interesting to us, and it's important we experience it at first hand to fully understand your world, which is the truth of learning, knowledge and wisdom.

As I started my connection with my life on Earth with Alexander, I had been prepared for various events that could happen during his life. Some of these would be things that would be placed on his path to help keep him in the love and the light. But I had also been told about the human need to sleep and eat, and their feelings such as anger, laughter, love, and part of this was the sexual feeling humans have for each other.

When I become part of a being that has gender, and humanity is one of these, I experience the passion of love and the sensations that arise in the human being around these feelings. It is sadly not always love, passion and kindness that arise around these sexual urges, it can also be unhappiness, betrayal, abuse, disappointment and even hate, when there is a breakdown in relationships. This was all new to me with Alexander. The first experience of his sexual urges was as a younger teenage boy when he liked a girl he knew, then as he grew into his older teen years I experienced his sexual urges again. When two humans come together to consummate a relationship, it's all very interesting for us, my friends, because other world beings we choose to connect with all have a different way of creating new beings. Of course, the human way is nurturing in the womb, which is how I merged into this world with Alexander.

As Alexander progressed into his teenage years, he learnt about his father's business and merchant traders in ancient Greece, and became familiar with the goods that were traded from his father ships. The ships travelled out into the Mediterranean carrying cereals, wine, olives, figs, pulses, eels, cheese, honey, meat, perfumes, tools and pottery. He learnt about the risks of ship trading, such as pirates, shipwrecks and the cargo going bad. Shipping also had good profit possibilities, as his father's wealth proved.

One of the experiences I chose to learn was to know the love of parents, which I did with Alexander; I also experienced his feelings about parenthood and bonding with his own children. He had an arranged marriage very common for the eldest son; it was important for him to marry into an upstanding family in the community that could enhance their own wealth and position in society. His wife was selected for him when he was a young boy; although he was not really aware of this until his teenage years, they knew each other, and were familiar to each other. If there was love there at first I did not sense it, but his love did grow for his wife, alongside respect for each other. You do still see this in modern humanities arranged marriages between women and men who do not have the freedom to find their true soul mates in life; all of you should have this choice, which would help bring more love and light into your world. But I do see it as an interesting part of human life, watching how you get on with what is presented to you and how you make the best of it. As for Alexander's feelings on this, he found it hard, but due to his great respect for his parents and heritage, he accepted this as his path in life.

Another thing I learned from being with Alexander was that humans have ambitions and dreams. One of the things I did want to learn from this physical connection was that you can have a passion and a dream to do something, which can be an urge since childhood. Alexander's was to join the army, and he had friends and a brother who also wished to do this. The time came in his late teens, when he was nineteen, when a couple of his friends decided to join the army, supporting the Roman Empire. There were still a lot of factions within the armies, some with the Roman Empire and some supporting those who wanted to overturn the Roman Empire. He did, as most boys would, play-fight and dream of being a soldier and saving the world. But often, as boys grow into young men, they start to understand what this can mean – leaving your home, not returning for years, and possibly losing your life. Although it was something Alexander wanted to do, at this time his father's health had started to decline a little, and it became obvious that the business would fall more on Alexander's shoulders over the next few years. He had to make the decision to support his family, and because of his character of honesty and devotion to his family, he chose this path. But he also held resentment within his heart; to be honest, I was surprised at the mixed bag of emotions and feelings around this, as it was something I had not experienced before.

Alexander was a very loving young man with a great sense of humour and a zest for life. He loved the outdoor life. As he started to grow into his teen years, he realised his life would have to be moulded by his father into his way of thinking, to run the family business. As the spirit within, it was funny to witness the human essence; he had strong will, had an ego, yet he had to submit to this way of being to support his family. At first he found this difficult, as his heart was elsewhere, dreaming of life in the army, dreaming of what was beyond this city he lived in, dreaming of another existence.

After his middle brother joined the army, he got on with his life, and because he got more and more involved in his father's business, he grew to accept his lot and soon moved on from the feelings of frustration. He was kept busy training his other brother to help with the business, but I did find him wondering sometimes what his friends were up to, and what might have been. I realised that dwelling on the past was a natural trait in humans. I remember the day well when his middle brother decided to join the army. It was hoped he would stay and help with the business, but being a bit of a rebel and of strong mind, he chose the army life. The day he left was full of grieving by his mother and sisters, as they did not know if they would ever see him again – there was not as much communication like there is in your modern day. People would leave never to be seen again, or return years later. Sometimes news could be passed by mouth or written message, which could take months to reach the families. Alexander's brother did return many years later, after his parents had passed on, and I remember him being so different to the young man that had left us behind. But this was the way of the world then, and very different to what you have now.

It was interesting as spirit within to witness the ambitions and dreams for the first time in the human mind. I realised humans had their own essence or human spirit, but your own essence is how we see it, combined with your own unique personalities, as we have too. As I saw Alexander mature, I witnessed aggression come in, especially in his late teens, a mixture of the male hormones and the knowledge that his future was set, even if it was not what he dreamed of. Sometimes, I saw him taking it out on other people, in fights with other young men, which did not sit well with me, but the continuous healing from his guides helped me deal with it. Experiencing all this human behaviour was such a massive learning curve. I realised his reaction was part of the human traits expressing supremacy, finding your path in life and not letting people bully you or put you down. As he grew into a young man and worked alongside his father, his aggression was channeled into the business; don't get me wrong – he was still a lovely young man but I could see he had spirit and he cared a lot for people around him. He also did not suffer fools lightly, and everyone knew where they stood with him, even his workers. He was strong in character, which I believe was stronger than his father's.

As Alexander grew into manhood, he realised that being a merchant was key not only to his own family's survival, but to that of many others in the city as well. This inspired him to help the merchant business grow and made the business more profitable and introducing modern changes in the way he used man power and storage of goods all helped with this.

At the age of 21, Alexander married Melissa; she was 16 years old, from a very respected family in Dyrrhachium. I discovered that each city had its own laws affecting marriage. In this case her father, the guardian, gave permission for Alexander to marry his daughter when she was a young child, and the agreement was made by the parents for a social and wealth match. Betrothing his daughter Melissa was seen as a gift and an alliance between the two households, and other gifts were also exchanged, including cattle.

They married in the January during a full moon, as this was linked to their belief of Hera, who was the sacred goddess of marriage, women, childbirth and family.

As time went on they had three children; they lost the first two pregnancies to miscarriage, and there was a time when they thought they would not have children, and this was hard, as they wanted male heirs to carry on the family lineage. But they were then blessed with two sons, Midylos and Lukos, followed by a younger daughter, Tryphosa. Alexander was very proud of his children and he took his sons under his wing, as his father had before him, to take over the business as they grew up. His father passed away when Alexander was in his late thirties; his father's body grew tired and a little weaker; one day he had a massive heart attack and he passed quickly. Because of his father's ill health, Alexander and his younger brother had taken over more and more of the business, so his passing did not affect their prosperity too much, but the loss of the physical essence of a loved one did leave a big hole in their hearts.

I thought you would be interested if I described the funeral process of this time to you. The people in Greece believed the funeral had to be done in a certain order so that the dead would pass through to the underworld.

The first part, the Prothesis, refers to the laying out and display of the body. Alexander's mother closed the eyes and mouth and placed a coin between her husband's teeth, which was payment for Charon, the ferryman of Hades. They believed the god Hades carried the newly deceased souls across the rivers Styx and Acheron that divided the world of the living from the world of the dead. Following this, his mother and sisters washed the body and dressed him in his finest clothes. Then they placed him on a bed in a central location in the house, and he was displayed so that loved ones and friends could come and pay their final respects.

The family held a formal mourning period out of respect for Alexander's father and gave relatives and friends time to pay their respects and mourn him. I noticed there was a distinction between the way men and women mourned. The chief mourner was Alexander's mother; she stood near the head and often held her husband's head in her hands in grief. The men that came typically did not show emotion and behaved in a formal and detached manner, while Alexander, as the new male head of the family, waited to greet guests some distance from the body. In contrast, the ladies that came stood near the body, wailing and gesturing wildly, including pulling at their hair. This was quite a sight to behold, I can tell you, but it was better for the physical body to let out the grief and emotions rather than holding it all in. Alexander held his emotions together as well as could be expected when in front of the other mourners, but I was pleased when he let them out when on his own, as I knew this would help him heal from his father's passing.

The body was then transferred to the place of interment in a funeral procession called the Ekphora. This took place at night and included multiple stops at intersections in the city on the way to the cemetery. The mourners attracted a large amount of public attention to honour the deceased, and I realised the stops were deliberate, a form of communication so all who knew the deceased could pay their respects. Then the family and friends went back to the family home for the Perideipnon, the funeral banquet. Unlike later Roman tradition, the Greeks did not imagine the dead partaking in the feast either with them or in the afterlife; instead, the feast was to celebrate Kleobis's life, which is what a funeral should be in my view, a time to reflect and remind everyone of the person they were.

When the funeral was over, offerings were made at the tomb on the third, ninth and 30th days after death, and on the one-year anniversary to give thanks to the gods. Some of these offerings included the sacrifice of animals, the donation of food and valuables, and a reprise of mourning by female family members.

It is interesting for us to witness the different burial methods and belief systems on Earth, but as we know, you all go back home to your point of origin.

The funeral of Kleobis was a sad day for my Earth friends, but with their beliefs in the underworld and their gods, grief did not last too long; as long as they followed the ritual of the burial, they trusted that their loved ones lived on in the underworld. The family accepted their loss well and moved on with their lives. Alexander's mother lived for another seven years after the death of his father. Her health started to fade over a couple of years. In your modern day you would call it cancer, but back then it was really unknown what was eating them away from the inside; the physicians could often feel tumours but a lot was unseen.

I would like to add a note here – cancer has been among humanity for a few thousand years, but on a very small scale, but we have observed in your modern world a massive increase – this is a man-made problem, mainly caused through stress, pollution, food, man-made drugs, alcohol and smoking. Your general poor health with heart disease and diabetes could all be eradicated – and will be in the future when you ascend. You will see there is a better way to live; there is no need for humanity to suffer like this. There are a lot of books to educate you in your world, please study them to improve your life styles and remember nature holds the key to your inner and outer well-being.

I did observe that losing his mother was a harder experience for Alexander than losing his father. I felt it was because of the bond with the mother that nurtured him for nine months, and also seeing her slowly weaken and fade away in pain. His experience with his father was sudden – one day he was gone, and his memory was of a strong man with occasional signs of weakness and tiredness. But his mother's ailing body, the weight loss and losing the strong person she used to be, was harder for him to bear. As the observer, it was hard for me to see all this emotion as well, and I had a lot of healing from my team at this time to keep me focused and pure of spirit.

We don't like to see a human or animal suffer, so for me, from the learning point of view, it was also interesting to see how the human body and mind reacted to all this and how Alexander bore it within his human essence and mind. I noticed he kept a lot of feelings inside regarding how he felt about his mother's illness; he was hurting and questioning why, which affected his physical body. The stress he endured made him more irritable than normal, and he was more tired than usual with broken sleep. After her death, he chose not to hold in this grief anymore and openly grieved for her. This was a great release for him and his energies cleared more to help him move forward, finding inner strengths to do so.

Wise words - It is important to give yourself time to grieve, days of solitude or with family and friends, because when you lose the physical presence of someone you love there is such an empty space in your everyday lives for you to adjust to. Remember that all of you need a different amount of time to go through the process of letting go. There will be anger, the why question, numbness, before you start to accept life without this loved one, adjusting at your own pace to the point where you can learn to live with the separation. Whether you have beliefs of an afterlife or not will depend on where you are in your world and spiritual development; but believe me, no matter what race or religion you all go come back home to your home world, dimensions or realms of existence.

Alexander lived with his wife in his family home with his parents; when his parents died he had to adjust to becoming the head of the household. I noticed that everyone living in the same home gave a support network and nurturing when needed, especially when losing a member of the family. I learnt this could be hard to adjust to for all the members of the household.

But as old energies left new came in, with, for example, the birth of children to his younger brother's wife, and so their lives carried on. After the death of his mother, Alexander was in his forties and his own children were growing up. His elder sisters Evgenia and Kallsto lived within the city, but his two younger sisters Myeine and Phaidra had married and left, so they had not been part of his life for a while. Through passing visitors, Alexander had heard word of children being born, but he did not see them often. A fact of family life in those days, I discovered, was that if you left your family group you often did not see them again, and there was a grieving process to this as we explained earlier when his brother left to join the army. There was not the communication like you have now that links the family bond through technology, but I saw the bond linked through the heart that could never be broken. There are still parts of your world today, perhaps more primitive in their way of being than yours, which thrive on those family groups. If you took time to study these communities, my friends, you would find healthier minds and spiritual beings, because they have the love and the support network of their close family group surrounding them.

Alexander progressed through his life working hard; he was caring, loving, generous with his time, and everyone knew where they stood with this honest man. He did not like the time wasters, especially on the business front, as time was precious in business and for money. The merchant business had expanded through his leadership, and his younger brother had proved to be a great asset in running their business affairs. Alexander was more the brains behind the business, while his brother Lukos was quite the adventurer and liked to go out on the ships searching for new merchandise to bring back to trade.

When Alexander reached his early fifties his wife became ill with the lung disease phthisis, which we know today as consumption. This was a time in the world where the human population started to move around more, and the more people that left their home shores and travelled, the more disease spread in all parts of the world. She suffered for a couple of years and eventually died from it, and this was another very sad day I witnessed in the life of Alexander. He stayed a strong, healthy man well into his early sixties until one day at his merchant yard, he was involved in an accident where some crates fell and he got caught under them. There were a couple of men injured; Alexander had broken a leg and was badly bruised and it took him a while to recover from this. To be honest, he did not ever fully recover from this accident and he was left with a limp and needed a stick for support. I witnessed how this slowed him down and how it frustrated him, because he was so used to being fit and active. I also witnessed the power of the mind, as Alexander's strong will for recovery and zest for life aided his healing.

At this time, his younger brother and his own two sons really stepped into the breach and took up more of the reins of running the business. This was an easy task for them, as Alexander had taught them well and they already had a lot of responsibilities. Alexander still had the brains but he soon realised he had to step back and let others run the business day-to-day. He would often go down to the docks to see what was going on there; he thrived on the busy port, especially when the ships returned home laden with their wares. I often witnessed the excitement he felt of the possible new cargos that his ships and men would bring when they were safely returned home.

Because of the family unit Alexander lived in he was never lonely, and as he grew older and spent more time away from the business, he actually enjoyed his time with his grandchildren, relaxing and watching them grow up. If any of you reading these words have grandchildren, you will know how much you can get from the love you gain from them. He realised it was OK to slow down, and place his trust in his brother and his two sons to carry on the business and the wealth of the family, to ensure their future support. He took pride in the fact that his own father had taught him well, as he had his own sons and brother. Alexander had achieved success in life because he was a great thinker and he could put things into perspective. He never realised he was connecting with us when he was doing this, and that his guides were guiding him with his thoughts, hoping his human self would listen, all at key times to help his Earth journey. Because he was a deep thinker, I had a great opportunity to connect more with him and help guide him, as well as really understand the human mind.

Alexander died in his early seventies, his heart grew tired, like his father's, and suddenly he passed. There were no outward signs, and he looked quite well right up to the end of his life, and was fairly healthy, apart from his limp and some pain from it. A few days before he passed he had some pain in his right arm. I remember this well as the observer, and I was of course aware we were approaching his time for passing and the end of my spirit within journey.

We prepare for this within the physical body, while my higher self and incarnation team prepare for the home-coming, the completion of the spirit within as I'm made whole again. We don't want the physical form to suffer, but with physical beings there is a point when the body stops in whatever form it is. We try to ensure the human essence does not feel a lot of pain, and there is a stage when they come unaware as the spirit within leaves their body, which is quite often just before they have taken their last breath. This was my first experience of separation from a physical being; I did feel a loss as I had been with this being for 74 years of your time. I loved him and I had grown to love everything about him, even the things I did not always understand, like the anger and frustration he sometimes showed. But as time went on, I came to understand the human form more and understand why you were what you were, and of course this was all part of my learning process.

As with the humans when a physical form leaves, and you miss their physical form and energy, I, too, missed being part of him and felt that I had left something behind that was part of me. But part of my healing when I return to the spirit realm is to let go of the emotional attachment of the physical form; I always will have part of Alexander's essence within me and in my memories. When I was healed, I looked at the life I had with him and what I had learnt, and the healing process helped me detach from my physical bond with Alexander.

I sat down with my healers and chosen guides for my journey and we looked at the timeline of this life, as we have said before, to evaluate it all and place in our knowledge pot, where it will serve others for the greater good in the future. We don't look at every second of the life line; I highlight wonderful memories, things that surprised me, wow moments to be viewed, and the learning points. As I was travelling this physical journey, other beings were also looking in on me from my family group. They all had their viewpoints and opinions on events in my life with Alexander and we all came to our conclusions on discussion points such as, for example, did I achieve what I set out to learn on this journey?

Nearly every time I have taken a physical life I have learnt so much more than I planned, and that is the amazing thing about this experience we choose to take. We don't just learn what we think we are going to learn, we learn a lot more than expected, and you can relate to this, my friends on Earth. For example, you go to your schools, colleges and universities to study a subject, say history, but while you are learning you will learn a lot more while on the path of knowledge. You learn about other people, their behaviour and cultures, how to interact with them, dedicate yourself and your mind to studying and so much more. Always think outside the box, as there is always something else to learn on top of what you think you are learning.

After my return home, I healed and carried on in my role as healer in my world; I did not forget about my existence with Alexander as I carried on in my life. I still remember and reflect on the journey I had with him, it never leaves me and is always part of me. But I don't let the times where there were emotion and sadness filter back into me; I see it all quite logically, quite openly, with the emotions detached from it. Think of Spock from your Star Trek movies, his character is portrayed as having no emotion and a logical way of thinking, yet the human part of him gave him soul and the humanity that was missing in his Vulcan DNA. I see it like this. Don't get me wrong, we do have emotions as a species, but we don't let them weigh us down; we have to separate ourselves from them and stay the pure light beings we are to carry on with our spiritual journey and ascension.

Conclusion – So what did I learn, as Ayderline the spirit within Alexander? I learnt what it was like for a physical body to function, develop and grow. Seeing the blood, organs and mind was part of my discovery of the journey I was undertaking. To help me with my journey, the understanding of the physical form was very key to this – how their minds and bodies work, how they cope with the different situations that arise in their lives, not just mentally, but physically too. This gives us greater understanding of that being and their race, especially if we choose to join again with their physical forms in the future. You see, when we are in our high ascended world, we see you as energy light beings, we know your personality and all your thoughts and feelings, so to connect closer is such a privilege for us and helps us to truly understand you. I also learned about human nature and different personalities, because even though I was spirit within Alexander, I could observe other humans as well. I loved to watch them as they grew from child to adult, their different characters and how they interacted with each other. I witnessed strong people and placid people, the ones that would be the natural leaders with power over others, and the people that would be the followers or victims. It was all very interesting, my friends, to observe this first-hand amongst any civilisation.

It was not just the interaction of humanity that fascinated me but the Earth animal kingdom as well. It was wonderful to see the nature of Earth. Yes, I was restricted to the area I was in, but I could leave Alexander's body, and when I did I took the opportunity to travel the planet and marvel at it. My favourite place was the seas and the barrier reefs created off the shores of tropical islands. I loved the vastness and contrast of various deserts and how they would merge with greenery, the cold areas of your planet and the beauty of snow and ice. I visited the individual civilisations to see how they were developing on Earth in this time-frame too; it was all very fascinating for me.

When Alexander would dive into the oceans of his coastline, I would see beautiful reefs, fishes and clear sea, and have the privilege to witness Earth unpolluted by modern man. Back in 403AD, men did put their waste into the water systems, rivers and sea, but because there were fewer humans and the vastness of the ocean, it was absorbed by nature. As you are aware, with the high population of modern man the Earth is not coping with the human waste you produce, and can no longer absorb it. I had learnt about your eco system and the way it works, the balance of nature necessary for all to survive. Alexander was living in a hot climate, very rarely was it cold; there was the odd time I witnessed snow, but on very rare occasions, and it was mostly warm to very hot weather. They had to preserve water in the hotter weather; a lot of their water was from springs from caverns below ground, where the water ran down off the mountains and hills. They also used the sea for bathing when the rivers ran low, and it was interesting to witness humanity surviving in the various climates around the Earth.

One of the things I witnessed that stood out to me was Alexander becoming a parent for the first time. It was a bit of a shock to him having a newborn child, mainly because of the rush of love he felt for this defenceless being, but the rush of love was awesome to witness. Humans have so much love to give, and you would be a very loving planet if only you could all allow yourselves to be like that. I saw a lot of love in that lifetime, because it was such a wonderful family-based unit in those days, living in a simple way. Yes, they had to survive and earn a living, and Alexander had responsibility for lots of people, but it was a simpler, slower pace of life. They lived within a time-frame back then, but they did not stick to it as much as you do in modern times. If anything, I felt they were a little a bit more ascended, as they accepted things would be done eventually and were not working to regimented time like you do now, so they took time to rest and play. They ensured their rest, especially in the hottest parts of the day, which you still do now in the hot parts of your world, where it's not too modernised with air-conditioning, and taking this time to rest makes sense.

This was all an education for me, how Alexander lived his life in that time-frame in Greece; as I said, I took the opportunity to go to other places on Earth, veiled so humans could not see me. The knowledge I picked up in the places I chose to visit was part of my journey and experiences as the spirit within. We are explorers within you as well as students. We love to explore, we want to learn, and we want to bring as much knowledge as we can back to our worlds.

As well as travelling the Earth, I explored the human body and mind. I came across emotions I had not experienced before; the one that was the hardest to deal with was hate. This was a shock to my system, and I had to find strength within my own spirit to cope with this connection with the physical form, as it is so different from anything we have experienced before. A key to me coping with this was the healing I received from my fellow incarnation team while I experienced these new feelings.

Another experience that stood out for me was when the time came to separate from the physical form; I was not prepared for the love I felt for him. I had been told what I might experience at separation, by my friends who had taken this path before me, but until you experience it yourself you never truly know. As my spirit within separated, I still felt attached to the physical plane of Earth, with what you would call feeling a little bit woozy, but this part of me was guided home by the spirits assigned to this task, and I was reunited with my higher self to be whole again. As we connected to complete the process, my healing spirit friends surrounded me and ensured all was well. I went through the debriefing healing process, joined by the healers and guides who accompanied me on my journey, and some of my spirit family group. I still had a lot of physical presence within me at this stage and felt a little bit lost without the human bond, but by the time the healing was complete, the bond was broken and I was left with memories. (Remember the explanations of the third, fourth and fifth dimension energies.)

Part of my healing process was listening to what the other spirits had to say about my journey with the human form. Because I was the spirit within, living this life with Alexander, I saw it from a different perspective. The others involved looked at it with no emotional attachment, so they had a clearer view of the journey I had just taken. I learnt from their feedback, knowledge and wisdom on events of this life we had chosen to focus on. All of this contributed to the conclusion of my journey, and what we decided to keep from this union with a physical being. Alexander was a strong, intelligent and positive being, with a sense of value instilled by his parents. I also knew he was aware of something else around him, an energy force he could not explain.

He never saw the divine spark and what we hoped he would recognise as the understanding of the divine overseers, but he understood right and wrong and he had love and empathy and these were important values we guided him to during his life. If he had chosen the path to the army, letting his ego come in, and allowing the strong side of his human essence to rule his heart, he would have experienced a more negative existence. This is because he would have seen a lot of death and trauma, and his experiences would have knocked his positive energies. So it was interesting to see the good side of life, and it was everything I wanted to experience and more. I wanted to experience a lot of positivity, seeing how humans adjusted to different situations, and this was an amazing first experience for me, choosing to be with Alexander in the physical form.

When the healing process was complete, I retained the love I had for Alexander and the memories of that existence. But I did not hold any negative emotions that might have occurred in that lifetime of bonding. We selected what was to go in the realm's knowledge pot for others to learn from, and when I felt ready I carried on with my life in my world. I returned to healing my fellow kind on their return home to us, and planned my next adventure. I felt that I had matured from this experience and the bond with the physical form. It had provided me with my next stage of knowledge and wisdom for ascension to the next level.

Chapter 3

Spirit within Ylva - *Earth*

I found my role as a healer fascinating because I was not just healing my fellow beings, I was also learning about where they had been and what they had seen. I took a mental note of the places I would like to visit; it was all so interesting, as all these various places were developing at different levels of ascension. I felt my time on Earth with Alexander had helped to give me a basic insight into what it was like being the spirit within the physical body of a different race of beings. It also had helped me start to better understand humanity and I wanted to learn more about you all.

I had been reflecting with my incarnation team about my life within Alexander, and had come to the conclusion that the life I had chosen with him had been quite sheltered. By this I mean he never went without anything and was mostly in a positive and stable environment. I felt that for my ascension progression, I needed to broaden my experience working with physical energies and with Earth, and part of this was to experience a harsher environment, a struggle for life and a different culture. By this, I mean the day-to-day survival of individuals, the struggle many humans have had in various parts of the world over the centuries. Those that survived were only the strong, while the weak perished; if you were weak, sickness took you quickly. People had to hunt daily for food and survive long harsh winters. Their whole focus was on building good shelters and food stocks to survive the winters, and key to this was the fire in their homes, for heating and cooking. It was an existence I wanted to experience; I could see it on the time lines, and even though I have a good imagination, I needed to live it to experience it. I thought Norway, which I had seen on my previous visit to Earth while out of my chosen physical body, was a very beautiful part Earth. I was attracted to its high mountains, fjords, crystal clear waters and seas, beautiful trees and wild flowers in the spring and summer. I was fascinated by the contrast and harshness of cold winters changing to hot summers, and it was such a beautiful country, even it was a harsher landscape to survive in than my previous experience in Greece.

When the time came to join with my new Earth energy, I blended with her the same way as I did with Alexander, but I need to explain here that when we link with different races and civilisations throughout the universe, we experience different energies for each one, and each individual Earth physical being also has their own individual energy stamp. To be scientific for a moment, this is based around your DNA and many generations of influences. Each time the energies of two beings come together to form another new being, a new energy being is created with their own individual energy vibration. No two beings anywhere in the universe have the same energy signature, not even your identical twins. Think of those human fingerprints, which reflect your individual energies; no two sets of fingerprints are the same. Because of this, we have to readjust with every single joining, never presuming this will be similar to another experience we have had.

I decided I would like to take another physical journey on Earth, and for this, we chose to be with Ylva, daughter of Devisser, in Norway in the ninth century of your time line. Ylva was born in the spring 912; I remember her birth being longer than Alexander's, and it was more effort for her mother Syivi to bring her into your world. I discovered birthing did not come easy to her; this is something I had observed, that it was not always a natural process for some humans, and could result in the death of the infant, the mother, or both. When Ylva finally merged into the world, she was a healthy crying little girl. There was much love from her mother for her, although sadly, I saw that her father had hoped for another boy; he did not have a lot of time for girls, he saw the sons as the future. But I observed that without the women, their sense of survival and life skills, there would be no mankind. I did, however, understand her father's feelings in the times they lived in, feelings that are still seen in parts of your world today.

Ylva's family lived in a fishing village called Rorvik, nestled among rocky slopes and cliffs, and was part of the Vikna archipelago, a municipality made up of about 6,000 islands. As well as fishing they farmed the many fertile lowland fields – these were the traditional ways of life for her people. She lived in what was called the Viking Age, a period of expansion by Scandinavian and other countries through trade, colonisation and the invasion of other countries to gain power over them.

This, my friends, was the time of the Vikings, and your modern day stories show them as being bloodthirsty, war-mongering people, adventuring forth and taking over continents. Many of them were like that, very strong races, but the community Ylva lived in provided food for their own village as well as others nearby. This was not easy, as other factions of their race could raid their own people for food. Here again, we see the survival of the fittest, making it a harsher day-to-day survival for them all. Because of this they trained their men and women to fight so they could defend themselves, hence the strong races that prevailed in the Viking period.

Ylva's father Devisser was a very well-known fisherman – his name even meant fisherman! He was often away at sea, which was a relief for the family, as he was quite an aggressive and impatient man, especially when he drank. Her mother Syivi was different, being of a quiet nature but strong in body and mind; her focus in life was ensuring her children's survival. In this time period, I saw that women could have great authority in the home and were respected by the men. But although Syivi's husband did not always show her respect, she held her ground and often won their battles, with her husband storming out. This created a household of many negative emotions for the family to live in, and I found it affected Ylva's energies.

Ylva was the middle child of five; she had an older brother Ake, and sister Dagmar, with a younger brother Eerikki and youngest of them all, her sister Inkeri; two other siblings had died as young babies before Ylva was born.

Her older brother Ake looked up to his father and being the eldest son, his father focused on him to help with the family and learn to be a fisherman; but Ake had other plans, as he dreamed of far-off lands. One day when he was in his late teens and his father was away fishing, he and couple of other young men packed up their belongings and left the village to seek their future overseas. Their families never saw them again, not even a word was carried to them of where they ended up and if they were safe. (Just to reassure you, I know they ended up in the far north of Scotland; they had joined a group of Vikings from Norway that were planning to raid and plunder. Ake settled in the Northern Isles of Orkney and lived his life out there.)

His father's heart was broken and he never recovered from the shame, as he had often bragged about his son and his fishing skills. Devisser was such a proud man, he did not understand this passion to leave the village and community, and the choice Ake made to never see his family again. Ake's chosen path also broke his mothers heart, but she also knew her son would never be happy while he yearned for adventure. Ylva missed her big brother too, as he made her laugh and teased her, but she had the insight to understand that Ake had to live his own life. When he was old enough, Ylva's younger brother Eerikki took on Ake's role; he was a different personality, more like his mother, and was quite content to fish and hunt and marry a local girl. Eerikki respected his father and the community's ways, so this was an easy decision for him.

The village Ylva lived in was made up of a group of low buildings with a central building for gatherings; to me, this felt as if it was more of a community way of living compared to what I had witnessed with Alexander. They lived in a long, box-shaped thatched roof house built of wood and stone. The walls were made of wattle, which was woven sticks covered with mud to keep out the bad weather. It was interesting learning how different parts of the world adapted to survive with the materials they had on hand. I witnessed such a simple existence; their home survival depended on keeping the fire going day and night, especially in the winter months, and this single Earth element would make the difference to them living or dying. As you know from your history, the discovery of fire over a million years ago was a major ascension point for humanity. This point in your history changed the direction of humanity's development, which was at the slow pace humanity could cope with. In Ylva's village, the children were taught to make fires from an early age; part of this was the responsibility to collect the firewood, under the watchful eye of their parents.

As you know, I wanted to experience a harsher environment to survive in and part of this challenge was the sourcing of food, and its quantity. During the summer months Ylva had quite a stable diet, but in the winter I saw that food could be rationed, and there were times when she would go to bed hungry. I witnessed that as a child she often cried herself to sleep because of a hollow feeling inside. At a young age she did not understand how she felt, but as she grew into her teen years and adulthood, she understood it was part of her existence, and acceptance came with this. I have to admit I did find these times hard to observe and I would give her healing with her guides to try and help her.

The main source of Ylva's diet was fish, meat from farm animals, and wild animals that they hunted, and they collected foods such as berries, nuts and honey. They cooked their meat in a big stew-pot over the fire, or roasted it on an iron spit. To sustain themselves over the winter months, fish and meat were smoke-dried to preserve it. They grew crops of rye and barley for their bread, cereal, mead and ale, and they also drank milk and used it to make cheese and butter. Interestingly they only had two meals a day, the early first meal was called the Dagmal or day meal, which mainly consisted of leftover stew still in the cauldron from the night before, with bread and fruit for the adults. The children would have porridge and dried fruit or perhaps buttermilk and bread, and this was usually served an hour after rising. The Nattmal or night meal was at the end of their working day; this could be fish or meat, stewed with vegetables. They might also eat some more fresh or dried fruit with honey as a sweet treat.

I witnessed the feasts they held in their community lodge at times of celebration such as weddings or seasonal festivals such as midwinter, where they ate very well and drank ale and mead. These were times when the community would come together to forget their day-to-day struggles and enjoy themselves, and it lifted the heart to see it.

I would say in general I witnessed quite a healthy diet, but it was the quantity of food available that caused struggle among them at times.

The village was sometimes raided for food, often by a small passing army or groups heading off to war or invasion. The village people had a choice to stand and fight or give over some food. Quite often, as the men were out at sea or hunting, the women were left to deal with these raids. They were usually threatened and forced to obey, but Ylva's village had lookouts and they had hiding places for food, to try and protect their own, which I thought was quite clever. They did often trade with other nearby communities too, which helped them build up their food stocks in what they lacked and vice-versa.

Here, I would like to tell you about Ylva's religion and its history to help you understand her village. They were pagans who worshipped the divinity of nature and they had many gods. Ylva's village had a chieftain who was also the equivalent of a priest, and the villagers' worship was focused around various gods; they would sacrifice animals, mainly horses, at times of celebration or to appease their gods.

Their history tells of gods and their relationship with giants, men and dwarfs. The most powerful god was the one-eyed Odin, the all father and god of warfare, justice, death, wisdom and poetry. Probably the most popular god, however, was Thor, who was not very bright yet incredibly strong. With his hammer Miollnir that was crafted by the dwarfs, he was the main defender of the gods against the giants. He was also the god of thunder, and seafarers particularly worshipped him. Amulets of Thor's hammer were popular throughout the Viking world, and used as weapons. The god and goddess of fertility were the brother and sister Frey and Freyja, they were also important and there were many other minor gods and goddesses too. Please note the element of giants and dwarfs and remember the elemental beings that choose to veil themselves from Earth for protection. A lot of these old writings are reflecting tales of long, long ago, passed on down the generations that came forth in the stories from their ancestors, who would have known elemental beings.

The burials I witnessed were often, in her village's case, in boats; they would have their prized possessions and anything they might need in the afterlife, which could include weapons, jewellery and food, and the boat was set on fire as it was pushed out to sea. If the passed person was poor and could not afford a boat, they were buried in a ring of stones shaped like a boat; the boat was important, because they believed it would carry them to the afterlife.

Remember The Greeks' mythology, and their gods; as with them, the stories of the Norse gods come from ancient times, of off-world visitors and elemental beings. Is it not fascinating for you, my friends? I wish there was more Earth evidence for you but so much has been lost. But when you return home, if you wish you can look at the time lines of Earth and see all this for yourselves. Anyway, because of their travels and invasions, the Viking people of foreign lands discovered Christianity, and as with the Greeks, it was not hard for the Norse people to absorb this new god into their way of thinking. Some eventually converted to Christianity and no longer worshipped the pagan way, but my time with Ylva was under the Pagan belief system.

Ylva was a very pretty little girl, with mousy, thick blond hair and big blue eyes; when she was happy she had a lovely laugh that people would stop and listen to. Laughter was lovely to hear, as we do love laughter in the spirit realm and we do love to hear all humans laugh and be happy, as it raises their energies. Up to the age of five, Ylva had a simple childhood which involved playing, she had a wooden doll she played with that had been carved for her by a kind neighbour. The children's playground was nature, where they raced each other, played ball games and had tugs of war. The children also had some shields and swords for play fighting. Remember this was a race with warriors in their blood and I saw it instilled in their children from an early age; and through the play the adults identified the defenders of the village, farmers and fisherman for their survival. In the home, Ylva learnt to do basic chores, such preparing food, collecting firewood, sewing and making medicines. The children could learn from observation, and she would watch her mother weave cloth for their clothes and embroider them, and when she was old enough she learnt this skill too.

The children would also learn to swim from an early age, and loved to swim in the summer months in the rivers and clear seas – it was a very popular pastime for all. As with Alexander, I enjoyed this pastime most of all, and Ylva was an excellent swimmer. They also used the rivers to wash their clothes and for general hygiene; in the winter it would be a stand-up wash in their home. It was very humbling to witness the simple existence of this time period; it was also very interesting to see how the children's imaginations could create games from simple things and their surroundings.

By this stage of her life, I realised that Ylva knew of no other way to exist. I knew it was the harsher existence that I had asked for compared to Alexander's life, but Ylva was unaware of any other existence that might be more comfortable and safe. It was all she knew, and she did not have the capacity to see beyond where she was in that moment of time, as we do in our existence - although she was a daydreamer, looking at the sea's horizon, and wondering what lands lay beyond it. Tales were told of other lands from the Viking invasions; this was a time when the young men would hear these stories and go off to far lands to fulfill their dreams, and Ylva heard these stories too. I discovered that nights around the fires in the house and village space were key times to talk and swap stories. Any family news was passed to the community and this social time was a nice contrast to their busy working days.

As Ylva grew up, she started to become more involved in the household duties to help her mother, which also taught her the skills she would need to run a home of her own one day. Their father taught the sons of the family to hunt and fish, as they were the main food providers. I also observed that at the time of the food harvest, all the villagers would help gather the crops in; it was important that all the community helped as this food was to share out among the families and for trade, ensuring their survival.

As her life progressed, Ylva's days were really all very similar, and as she got to her teenage years, so much was expected of her and she was kept very busy with the household chores. She had become a very good sewer and her embroidery was exquisite for the time. This was also her passion, and when she had a quiet moment she would take herself off somewhere to sew. In the summer months you would find her under a large tree a little way from the village, in a field of wild grass and flowers that she loved. It was on one of these occasions, when she was fifteen years old, that she met her future husband Stian. He was 19 years old, from a nearby community in the group of islands, and had come to trade some of his father's tools. Stian and his father were fishermen and in the winter months when they were not at sea, they made tools to trade. I'll never forget the first time they met, as this was their destiny, they chatted for a while and started to meet up when Stian visited the village. It was interesting to witness as the spirit within the first pangs of true love, her daily thoughts were filled with him and she sang to herself through the day. I found this was an uplifting experience and it made me realise that no matter how hard a day can be for Ylva, true love can take all the doubt and pain away.

Well, their relationship grew and the two families approved of the union and agreed to their marriage, which took place in the summer of 928. The wedding was held in her village and overseen by the leader of the community, who acted as a priest type figure for marriages and funerals. It was a day of great rejoicing, eating and drinking; the only sad part was really for Ylva's mother and siblings, as Ylva was going to live in her husband's village on the nearby island Storvollen. I have to admit Ylva was so excited that she did not really think about this, and she knew her family was not really that far away from her.

With the help of his family, Stian had built a home for them, and Ylva was looking forward to her future with this young man. It was important for the communities that the women were still virgins when they married, as this brought a higher standing to the families and was important for the couple's future. As she was still a maiden, I remember that Ylva's wedding night was a bit scary for her, not really knowing what to expect from their union. She had seen naked men from a distance when bathing, and had chatted with her older sister about what happens between a man and woman, but had yet to experience physical love for herself. Being the spirit within and experiencing a union based on love was so different to Alexander's marriage-night union, which was with a woman he respected but did not love. The difference here was true love and it was a happier wedding night for Ylva with laughter and passion, and all that mattered to her was the love they shared.

Ylva set about making a home for them both, her embroidery and sewing starting to fill their little lodge, and she also discovered she could trade her work for other items as people appreciated her skills and eye for design. Stian spent many a long day out fishing, but Ylva was used to this life, having come from a fishing family. The village, although smaller, was similar to her home village and Stian's family made her welcome. She was very happy for this time period. As usual, in the background survival was at the forefront, but her happiness outshone any concerns. The first five years of marriage were very happy, the only damper being that they had hoped for a child and there was still no sign of one. They began to wonder if she was barren, but hope still remained as their love was strong and gave them faith all would be all right in their future. The thought of being unable to have children at this time did not really bother them; it bothered other people surrounding them more, as children were the future of their community.

Then the day of great change arrived. It was late autumn in the year 933, the fishing fleet had gone out early, and as the day progressed a storm came rolling in – the fishermen including Stian had not known when they set out that there were storms way out at sea. The fleet of three boats got caught up in the storm, pushing them away from land and eventually capsizing the boats, with the loss of all lives. Back at home, the weather was stormy with rough seas but they were unaware of what had befallen the boats and by the next morning, the villagers were getting worried. As they had not returned, a couple of boats went out to search, but could not find any sign of them. The village did not lose hope, as there had been cases of boats coming back after a couple of days, when the fishermen had taken shelter somewhere, and so they waited. Ylva went up to the highest point above the village and sat, looking out to sea for a glimpse of her beloved, but he did not return.

This is when it gets tough for the spirit within, as we knew his fate; it was his time to return to us. We had to wait out the time it took for Ylva to realise this, and be there with love and healing to try and help cushion the blow of her loss. I was quite taken aback at how badly she took it, she would not accept it straightaway and spent many hours searching the horizons, but gradually it dawned her that he was not coming back. She felt so empty inside; she wished she had a child to cradle so she had something of him to hold onto. I saw her become desolate and lonely, withdrawing into herself; her energies were so low we found it hard to give her healing, but we kept trying. Eventually she chose to stay in his home village, always hoping one day he would return. She would not accept another marriage and rumours had abounded she was barren, so men soon left her alone. She then settled into her isolated existence, surviving through her sewing skills, trading clothes and embroidery for food and whatever else she needed. This was a time when people valued clothes and often used them as gifts or a dowry upon marriage. It was because of these skills that the village elders allowed her to live out her days with them. This was a kind act because if a widow was not offered marriage, she was expected to return to her home village, and not place a burden on the village resources.

The years passed, and in this time frame Ylva lost her parents, but really felt no emotion. Sometimes her siblings would come and see her, but they soon stopped. People started to think of her as the crazy lady, as she often talked to herself for comfort, trying to hold onto the memories of her beloved Stian.

It did sadden us, but her path was set and I had to accept this, because I had asked for the harsher reality of life as well as a harsh living environment. It had not dawned on me how much loneliness and heartache there would be in this physical being's existence. My incarnation team was busy giving me healing as I had not experienced anything like it, and I was busy giving Ylva healing. But sadly, I don't think in the latter years of her life she felt it. She grew old for her years, white-haired and frail, and at the age of 49, she started to fade. Her inner wish was not be on the Earth plane any more, secretly believing she would meet her love again – and of course, she was right. All we could do as her spirit within support team was make it as easy for her as we could; the last few days of her life were drawn out with laboured breath and pain. One day, I told her it was all right to let go and calmed her, and she then took her last breath. I remember that as I was released, I had an overwhelming feeling of relief to leave this Earth life, away from this life of loneliness that had been created from lost love.

Conclusion - When I was spirit within Ylva and being part of living in a harsher reality of daily survival, it hit home how different this was to my previous Earth experience. The main difference was the love – there was not much time for it when she was growing up. I saw her receiving love from her mother but this was rarely, as her mother was so busy surviving because day-to-day living was very hard. Her father was a man who did not show much love and kept his feelings private. He did not bring much love into the house, really only fear of his anger, which mainly came forward when he was drinking alcohol. But Ylva did receive the love of her siblings and they all had a common bond, to look after each other and survive.

I saw that this sort of environment affected her human energies, keeping them low and deflated a lot of the time. It was at this point in time I saw clearly that our mission to bring love and light to all beings, to help them ascend, was going to be harder than I thought. This is because when your energies are low and negative it blocks out the higher ascended energies of the spirit realm. I realised that if Ylva's reality changed, her physical energy would be stronger, and she would be more hopeful and happier; until then, I would not be able to bring this love and light to her as spirit within. This feeling of not fulfilling my role came to me quite soon after my joining with her, as I could see the world around her had low energy. Then I realised that I was actually judging this based on moments in time while in Earth's reality. I knew I must not give up on this human and her human essence, and I would always strive to give her the love and the healing she needed while she carried on with this journey. There were times during her life when all her guides and myself would pull as close as we could into her energy, to surround her with love and ease her pain. We know that some of this healing would penetrate her energies to help her, even if she was unaware of it.

Then I experienced the six years of love Ylva held for her husband, a love of the heart and soul. This lifted her energies to a higher energy plane. Sometimes she sensed something she did not really understand, but in those moments she was comforted, and that's what mattered to us. But even then, I don't think she ever realised we were there, even when she would feel a bit comforted with the love. Then there were her years of heartbreak and loneliness, and even though I had chosen the harsher reality to experience, I felt it was something I did not want to experience again, as it saddened my heart and saddened my inner being. I found it hard as the spirit within to hold my love and light energy all the time because of the suffering I was seeing this human go through. Yes, I did see suffering while with Alexander, struggle and grief, but Ylva's was a different type of struggle, a deeper struggle for daily survival from the day-to-day fight of mind, body and soul. Don't get me wrong, I did witness moments of happiness, and rejoiced after her husband passed back home to us, but these were few and far between, at a time on Earth in this part of the world when the energies were lower, and the people were more aggressive and wanted to dominate each other. So you can understand, my friends, when we talk about bringing our love and light to the world and penetrating Earth's energies when they were lower, it made it harder for us to connect with you. I had had a de-briefing before I came to join this Earth life and knew it would be harder, but didn't understand how hard until I experienced it.

I hear you ask, why put yourself through this experience if you have a choice? The one thing I did realise is that we need to experience to understand the human ego and human essence. This then helps us know the extent of the work we and other ascension beings have to do to bring humanity towards the ascension level of unconditional love and light. I realised how far away we were from this and it was a bit of a reality check for me as the spirit within. So one half of me did not want to experience this type of reality again, but the other half knew that for us to help humanity ascend, we would need to experience all types of dark, harsh realties to bring the love and light forward into your world. This is so the next generation does not have as much darkness in their world to contend with. Wow – what an amazing learning curve it was for me!

Chapter 4

Spirit within Eliza – *Earth*

After my life as spirit within Ylva I had the healing time I needed to adjust my energies on my return to my world, and then carried on in my healing role. I felt these experiences were aiding my ascension process on my home world. I should explain that as we ascend, our consciousness expands, bringing with it an all-knowing clarity which builds on each ascension level I take. I suppose the best way to explain this is that while we all work in unity, we are also self-focused, and with each ascension stage I increasingly started to look at the bigger picture beyond myself. This meant I would not just focus on my own journey, learning and pathway as I moved forward with my life. My growth had brought me to a point where I could also see how others would be affected by the chosen physical existences they had taken and on the planets, realms or dimensions of my choice.

One of our values is: All thoughts and actions are for the best outcome for all involved, and this is taught from our earliest teachings to us. This is vital as we have access to so much knowledge, and we need to be fully aware that all actions and thoughts create consequences. As we reach the higher levels our conscious energy starts to grow and expand, bringing great telepathic connections that can reach beyond our physical world. This means that I always have to check my actions, any decisions I make, and the effect they have on others, as they cause a ripple effect throughout the universe. Every thought you have has this power too – remember that thoughts are energy, and how you think affects your life and those of others.

I reflected about all this with my incarnation team and they thought I was ready as part of this new ascension growth to take on a physical being existence that was different to the last two. My new physical life would be more for lessons for others than myself, and this will come clear as the story unfolds. This would lead to my passing, which would be more of a lesson for those 'spirits within' left behind rather than for me. The lessons are their reactions to certain events of my next physical life and the learning they sought on their own life paths. I would learn from all this too, but it was as if I was playing out a scene on a stage for the audience to react to and make their own interpretation of the play.

My next place for a physical being choice was Earth again, in the early eighteenth century, where Eliza Mary Thomas was born in 1703. I witnessed an easy pregnancy and quick delivery as she came bouncing into the room – they had to catch her as she entered the world as she left her safe cocoon of her mother Mary's womb. I have to say what a miracle this is to witness, and even though this was my third time of connecting with a physical being, it was still an amazing experience. Eliza was a little shocked and tired as she entered the world, as all babies are, but being kept warm and safe the womb was soon forgotten. I remembered that when I joined with Eliza and connected to the world around me, there was a lot of excitement around the mother and father at the prospect of their first child. Mary was much loved by her husband Joseph and all who knew her; she had a wonderful, sunny disposition and was pretty, with rosy cheeks and a huge warming smile for everyone. Mary was a natural mother and loved Eliza very much. I did sense from the father the hope of the first-born being a son, but his wish was soon granted when their second child Joseph, named after his father, came along 13 months later.

Eliza was the eldest of eleven children and sadly, she lost her mother Mary after she gave birth to her eleventh child Ann in 1720, due to an infection. It was hard to watch the fever ravage her body, and for a while there was hope she would pull through, but she was too weak after a difficult birth and blood loss, and after 10 days she passed away. As this was her eleventh child and they all expected it to be an easy labour, her death was a shock, but Ann was a big baby and a breach birth, which caused tearing, loss of blood and infection. Mary was unconscious for the last couple of days of her life, and her spirit within was preparing to leave. I could see all of this and we communicated; we all made sure the human part was pain free, even though to the outside world she looked as if she was suffering.

It was hard to witness, but interesting to study the shock and the void this woman left in the family's lives, and it took a while for the laughter and joy to return to this previously happy home. When it did return, it was mainly through Eliza's hearty way of being that helped them all move forward out of grief. Eliza learnt to suppress her grief in front of her siblings, to try and bring back the happiness they had known. But she had times when she would take herself off to a quiet place to grieve, where the others would not see. This would often be at the end of the day, when her mind had time to think of her darling mother Mary. Eliza's beliefs of life after death were unsure in her heart; she rarely visited the local church, as religion was not at the forefront of this family's thinking. After her mother's death she would often reflect how short life can be, and how important it was to try to make the best of every moment. I know that sometimes Eliza felt our closeness; it gave her comfort but she had no clear belief either way, and simply felt you had to make the best of what you have and enjoy life while you can. We felt she had a very natural, spiritual way of being and if alive in your modern day, she would have had a spiritualist understanding of what she felt, but she lived in an era when this was not recognised.

In total in Eliza's family, there were six girls and five boys. Next in age to Eliza was Joseph, then John, the twins Victoria and Margaret, then Walter, Matthew, Grace, Alice, Richard and Ann. They all lived on a large farm near the market town of Dorking in Surrey. The farm was just known as Thomas Farm, and had been in their family for three generations. They had cattle, sheep, goats and chickens and grew crops to feed themselves and their livestock through the winters. I thought the farmhouse was impressive, compared to other dwellings I had experienced while on the Earth plane. It was stone built with a thatched roof and was made up of two floors; outside the farmyard, there was a large barn and small outbuildings scattered around. It was a lovely, cool, airy house in the summer months but it was hard to heat in the winter, and the kitchen became the centre for gatherings around the big, blazing fire.

There was a huge kitchen table in the centre of the room, which was a wonderful place to be part of at meal times for the family and farmhands. I was kept very busy observing this family, because there was never a dull moment on the farm. Chickens running loose being shooed out of the kitchen, the goats eating things they shouldn't, the two Lurcher dogs always looking for that hidden scrap when Eliza's back was turned. I must not forget the cats, bringing in their gifts of mice and rats for Eliza, which was nature's balanced way as I observed it. When she could, Eliza brought flowers into the home, as she loved flowers – especially wild flowers, which she picked in the summer to place on the highly scrubbed kitchen table. I was a very happy spirit within, just sitting back and watching this happy, simple energy space, which was Eliza's home.

Being the eldest, Eliza had always been the equivalent of a second mother to her siblings. They were all quite a handful and Mary was grateful for Eliza's help with their washing, dressing and general welfare, and help with the household chores. It was a happy family farm, even though it could be tough at times of hardships and survival, but in my opinion, it was a lot easier than Ylva's life experiences.

Farming in Eliza's time was for the long-term survival of them all, as well as for the people of the town and surrounding villages who relied on their milk, beef, lamb and wool. Farming could be a tough livelihood, but her father was a progressive thinker and was looking at changing the way they farmed. He had already included crops for hay, animal feed and their own food, and had expanded to sell crops to the flourmills as well. Joseph was a true lover of the land and a very hard-working, honest man with a big heart. He was tall and broad-shouldered man, good-looking in a rough-round-the-edges way, and commanded great presence and respect in the local community. He was one of those men who lit up every room he entered, with a deep, booming laugh that always made me smile inside. He was a fairly strict father and had great affection for his children, but they knew their boundaries and were brought up to understand that as their livelihood, the farm came first. Eliza had a great love and respect for her father and she appreciated his support after her mother's death, when he respected the decisions she had to make for the children and the household.

The first 17 years of Eliza's life were very happily spent within her busy family farm life. She was what you would call a bonny girl; she had dark brown hair, hazel brown eyes and rosy cheeks, and was very much like her mother in appearance. Her heart had the capacity for much love, which I felt shone out from a young age – not just for humans but for the animal kingdom, too. Even though she was a farmer's daughter, she did not like to see any harm come to animals; she had to learn to accept that animals were killed for food, so she just made sure she did not witness this.

The farmhouse was quite big, but the children did have to share bedrooms. When she was little she shared her bedroom with her siblings, but as more were born and they got older, the bedrooms were divided between boys and girls. For many centuries, I had seen that unless there was wealth in the family, everyone lived and slept in the same rooms without much privacy, although Eliza was lucky enough to eventually just share with her sisters. This was a time when many people were still self-sufficient by making their own clothes, weaving cloth and knitting. The advantage of being the eldest was that Eliza got the new clothes, then they were handed down to the other female siblings and nothing was wasted. Because of her kind personality she felt guilty about this, and after her mother died she made sure the others got new clothes when needed, while she adjusted her mother's clothes and reused them. Their general hygiene meant body washes; they had a basin and jug in their bedrooms, and the tin bath was filled once a week, which everyone shared. There was also a large stream near the farm that they liked to bathe in, in the milder weather. When Eliza took over the care of her siblings, one of biggest challenges was keeping them clean, as I saw that a farm was a mucky and smelly place to live.

Because of the busy life she led, Eliza did not always have a lot of time to herself, and when she did you would find her somewhere on the farm, day-dreaming of a life beyond it, away from the day in, day out life of chores, and a future of marriage that she knew would take her to another farm over the horizon. I loved it when she would go on one of her wanders, picking flowers and finding somewhere to sit, just reflecting on her day and watching nature. She loved it when butterflies would come and land on her; this was actually us making this happen as it brought her much joy. This is a lovely time for us to connect with humans, as they connect with the Earth energy, and we always brought calm and healing to Eliza at these times. For a human to be close to nature brings you close to the spiritual way of being in your heart and mind, connecting you closer to the spirit within.

As well as looking after her siblings, Eliza helped around the farm milking cows, and taught the younger children her chores when they were old enough, because everyone had a part to play in farm life. Like most girls, she had a dream of marrying one day, but when her mother passed away in the early spring in Eliza's seventeenth year, she found herself looking after the children and a newborn baby; they were so dependent on her, marriage was forgotten. I remember the heartache and shock in the family that their beloved mother had gone, her father Joseph was quite taken aback, he thought his wife was invincible and could only see a future where they would grow old together. In this heartache, he took it for granted that Eliza would take over her mother's role with the children, and they found a nursing mother in the village to help with feeding the baby. This did help give Eliza more time with the other siblings, but as I witnessed, it was not just making sure they were fed, clean and doing their chores, but comforting them over the loss of their mother as well.

In the summer of Eliza's seventeenth year, she did have a little secret romance with a summer farm worker who helped on the land and with the harvests. Peter, a handsome, fair-haired young man, brought romance to her life and love's first kisses. He often gave her bunches of wild flowers, causing much amusement among her siblings, and this fuelled her dreams of what life could be if she married. This romance was designed as distraction for them all on her life's path, to help them realise that life carried on. But at the end of the season, Peter moved on to find work in the city of London during the winter months, and she never saw him again. He was often in her thoughts and she wondered what had become of him; she thought he would return the following spring, but never did. (For your curiosity, Peter died of fever early the following year in London; he was ill-nourished and the fever was sweeping the city and taking the weak. He could not read and write so he sent no letters to Eliza, and the news of his death never reached her.) You might think, why could Eliza not marry? When she took on her mother's role, she was left with little time to meet men; on top of that, she was not such an attractive proposition, surrounded by so many siblings. Often, following the wedding, the bride would go to the husband's home, or they would set up on their own and as you have probably realised by now, this was not written into her path, so it was not her destiny, my friends.

I would like to talk about the religion in Eliza's time period. Her family did not have any great enthusiasm for religion – they had emerged from the 17th century, where the Catholic religion had been cleared from the lands, so this was the time of the Protestants. We saw it as more of an age of reason for humanity, after witnessing over 150 years of civil movements and wars over religion in England and Europe. I felt humans in this part of the world had lost their way; the divine spark was no longer part of religion, it was power and wealth that was sought. I also felt the churches lacked vigour and drive after the years of fighting within the faith, there was a tiredness of religion, whilst for many, the understanding had got lost. We had to work hard to try and guide humanity towards recognising the divine spark again. I'm not sure we have yet, but with the birth of spiritualism on Earth, we now see a clear road forward to bringing back that divine spark for all.

As well as a happy disposition, Eliza was also very creative and was an artist. When she had the opportunity and money allowed, she would buy paper and ink and do little sketches of farm life and flowers. I feel that if she had lived in your day and age she would have been a very creative, artistic person. She was also a very bright young woman but she was limited by her background and time line; she kept a lot of these talents hidden, as in those days, women were not expected to be anything but homemakers. Her pastimes were expected to be sewing and weaving - although she did have those skills as well, and passed them on to her younger sisters, they were chores to her, not a joy. None of the children were educated so none of them could read or write; this limited their futures and the farm life or service in a wealthy house were their only options of making a living.

I can quite honestly say that Eliza did not have a bad bone in her body; her kindness radiated round her, she accepted her lot and worked hard. She spent most of her time in the farmhouse kitchen preparing meals, washing the children and running the farmhouse while her father was working on the land. Even though siblings and farm-working adults surrounded Eliza daily, I often felt loneliness inside her, but she did confide in her brother Joseph, the eldest of the sons. She was also pleased when he married a village girl called Maisie; when she came to live at the farmhouse, Eliza welcomed her with open arms. As well as an extra pair of hands, it gave her someone new to talk to about life as a whole. She was so happy for her brother, as was her father, and they all looked forward to the tiny patter of feet of future children.

Not long after her brother's wedding in the summer of 1724, Eliza passed away, and my time with her was over. The family farm had a big barn, which housed some livestock such as nursing cows and horses when they were not in the fields. It was also a food storage area, a place for the hired farm workers to sleep, and a play area for the younger children. One hot summer's day while Eliza was in the kitchen, she heard shouts that the barn was on fire. She could not understand how this could happen, but she ran out, seeing the smoke and flames at the corner of the far end of the barn. Her father and brother Joseph were visiting a nearby farm to look at a breeding bull, so she was in charge. She shouted to those around to form a queue and get water from the well to try and stop the flames, and then she had to locate some of the children, as she could not see Grace and Alice. She rushed into the barn without thinking of herself, and could see the flames in the corner, creeping up the wall towards the roof. She found the two frightened siblings near the haystacks with a cat and kittens that were only a couple of days old and they did not want to leave them, so Eliza scooped up the cats and got the girls out of the barn. She could then hear a couple of lame horses and a cow with her calf crying in fear, and ran back in to save the animals. She managed to get the livestock out and one horse with the help of a couple of farmhands, and checked there was no-one else in there, instructing Maisie and the older siblings to round up the children outside, well away from the barn.

By this time the horse left in the barn was neighing very loudly and obviously scared. We were being kept busy by all of this, as we tried to calm the animals and humans with healing. Eliza then went back to get the last horse; even though the others were telling her not to go back in, she could not bear the thought of the horse suffering. By this time the flames were starting to lap across the roof, and smoke was starting to fill the barn, with bits of the burning roof dropping down and spreading the fire. I could hear the heat of the flames spitting and the cracking of wood. As she released the last horse, which ran for the open barn door, part of the roof fell and a large ground support beam landed on her left-hand side, trapping her. I could feel the fear in her and the realisation she might die. She was only conscious for a few minutes before the pain and smoke knocked her out, and then the fire consumed the barn and Eliza with it. We made sure she did not know any pain after that as I left her and her human form passed away. This was quite a traumatic passing I have to admit, compared to my two previous death experiences, and I moved away from the Earth energy plane very quickly so I did not witness her being burnt. I was met by a close friend of mine in incarnation team, and a couple of her permanent guides also helped me back home.

As you can imagine, this was a very traumatic experience for all who witnessed this event. Even in the shock of her death, those that knew her well would know she would have put everyone else first before her own safety. Eliza's death was very hard for all the family, not just losing her but because she passed in a very tragic way, and in their thoughts, they always wondered if they could have done more, or stopped her, and she might still have been alive today. Her father and brother felt such guilt being away from the farm when this all happened, but remember, my friends, there are things in life you cannot change, even though the human mind and human essence does not always recognize this, depending on your beliefs of life and beyond.

I observed from my home world the day of Eliza's funeral, and saw that the laughter and light had been extinguished from the family. The heaviness of the energies was very overpowering, making it hard for me to study and learn properly. I chose to observe this, as it was an interesting lesson in energies for me. When we choose to work with humanity, as a whole or individually, the energies on Earth or within individuals affect this. For example, the first and second world wars on Earth were hard times for us; it took everything we had to keep working with each human, healing and guiding as best we could. It was like a dark shroud placed over Mother Earth. Now, especially in the last 30 years or more, as the enlightenment is coming into Earth and more and more of you are becoming light workers or truly spiritual, the energies are lifting and vibrating out into the universe.

When it started to hit home to her family that their Eliza had passed away, it started to dawn on the now oldest daughter, Victoria, one of the twins who was now 12, that it was now for her to take over Eliza's role within the household. But as she was still so young, Joseph's wife Maisie took on this role, with Victoria and her twin sister to help, and this meant they had to grow up very quickly. Joseph realised how much talking with Eliza had helped sort out their worries, and how much wisdom she had for such a young woman and he had now lost his confidante. They all had to step up to their chores, and they felt a little guilt, as they had all taken advantage of Eliza's kind heart. Her father was visibly shaken by her death for a long time, losing two women he loved in different ways in just four years was a hard blow for his heart. He was silently proud of her bravery on the day of the fire, and thought many times that a barn can be rebuilt, but you can't replace Eliza.

Conclusion - why did I choose this life, to be the spirit within Eliza? As I mentioned at the beginning of her story, this was a life from which lessons would be learnt by the people close to her, the spirit within them, and the student. It was almost as if Eliza was set up as the leading lady, setting the example to others with her kindness and selfless acts, to be applauded by all – but only after her death was her performance recognised for its worth.

Eliza had a simple existence, and I wanted to experience being part of a large family, having lots of siblings, and the laughter and the fun this can bring, outweighing the mundane life of these times. Eliza had a very gentle human essence; she had a huge capacity for love, she was a daydreamer, a secret talented artist; if she had had the opportunities in life your modern day could bring her, her talent would have shone.

I knew it would be a shorter life with this physical being but I wanted to experience the same day in, day out routine – how do humans cope with a repetitive way of being, living in the restricted third dimension existence? I look at my life and it varies so much and I'm not restricted by your third dimension energy plane, I don't have the time restraints of the human life and I'm also capable of being in more than one place at once through my mind conscious state of being – can you imagine this kind of living, my friends? I must point out that every human DNA is different, so I can pick six different beings, in the same life scenario, but with each human I would experience a different way of being because their human essence would be different.

Eliza was a key member of her Earth family, and this was shown to me by the way she was respected by those that lived on the farm and those who came to visit. After her mother died when her father was not around, she was the next person everyone looked up to and went to for help and advice. As I have already said, her life was simple, the family knew no other way, they saw riches from afar that belonged to the gentry in the area, but the country life was what they were born into and was in their blood. I did notice the class difference in this lifetime; there was more of an extreme difference between the poor, the middle class and the rich. It was interesting to us to see how Earth beings had let this happen, rather than making sure all were fed, clothed and cared for in a world of unity. For example, in Ylva's community, there were the elders, but none lived better that another, as it was all about surviving as a community compared to this time line of Eliza's. This is something I really started to take note of, how humanity still lives by these standards even in your modern societies. But I know one day this will be eradicated from your world as you ascend into beings with greater understanding for all of humanity.

Eliza's family found it a big shock after losing their mother and then Eliza, as they were both key figures in their lives, and as I have already said, all her siblings found themselves on a steep learning curve. Their path from her death was to accept her loss and learn to adjust to losing these two women who had held their family together. They also needed to reflect on their own life paths so far, to pick themselves back up, become better people and survive. Eliza had often thought she could not leave her home to marry until at least the eldest girl Victoria was ready to take over, and then she also thought that it would not be fair to restrict Victoria's life, because she was always thinking of others. She had already arranged for a couple of the older children to work a few days a week in the house of some local gentry, as the farm did not always pay its way and they had to earn their way and contribute to the family. Eliza did find this hard as she felt guilty, but needs must, and it was very common in those times for younger family members to go to work, especially when there were 14 people to feed plus workers – every penny counted.

It was good for me to experience this working life and I observed little comforts; she had those moments by the fire to herself doing a sketch, hiding her pen and paper, as this was money spent she could not perhaps afford. This was one of her few selfish acts, but she did feel guilty as only a human can, as she was trying to keep everybody clothed. Nearly all their clothes were made by the farm women; a few items were bought from the local town. I remember that every year, there was a trip to the market in the nearby town; they would all dress up in their best clothes, and with her hard-earned money, Eliza would treat herself to a piece of hair ribbon. Everyone would have a treat, and I saw that this was a major event of the year, for which they would have saved all year for. This was the type of life I wanted to experience**, which appreciated the little things in life.** The simplicity of life and the gratitude for receiving something like a ribbon were precious in those times.

I must not forget the lesson for all those that knew Eliza: because of her happy personality and because she gave so much out to others, they all took her for granted. Eliza would rather see her siblings have some fun, and take on an extra chore so they could do this, but it was rare they offered to help her unless she asked, when they all knew what was expected of them. But they would often let Eliza do their chores so they could have more pleasure. It made her smile to see them have the simple pleasures in life, and the love she felt for her family meant she put their needs before her own. This is something I have witnessed in all my Earth encounters – the way humans can take others for granted. I see this as a selfish act, putting your own needs first, so think, my friends, before you do this, think of others before yourself, as it is the acts like taking others for granted that hold back your ascension.

Reflecting on it now, I have to admit that I was enlightened by this life as I got a glimpse of a human at their best, and we know that if all of humanity could be more caring and loving, what a wonderful world you would live in. Remember the different dimensions I mentioned; raising the energies would mean there are no conflicts, and there would be acceptance of all, the animal kingdom would be cared for rather than extinguished, and the wounded Mother Earth would be healed.

What I have not mentioned before is that after my physical life has ended and I have healed my energies in my world, I do sometimes look in on the time lines to see how the other members of that existence are getting on. This was especially so with Eliza's life, as it was a lesson for the others to learn from. Some of these spirits within I helped heal on their return, as I had a great understanding of the path they had lived and the lessons they should have learnt while in that physical existence.

We know that when a life ends young it is hard for a human to reason why. We do hear your voices and the thought that when a child or young adult is taken back too quickly, you seem to think it is before their time. We hear your questions for example: Why so young? Why did they not live a full, long life? It's because their passing is for lessons to be learnt by those left behind. One example of this would be a child passing young, which seems a senseless loss - why could they not live their life out to the full? I know if you are reading this and have lost someone at a young age, it's hard for you comprehend this. But take a look around you and see how your lives intertwine; these events are all planned and guided into the path they need to be on. There are times when a young human or adult can be in deep depression, as if they are in a deep dark cave with no light and there is no way to climb out. The depressed physical human body will have the lowest energies and sometimes there is no way for spirit to get through to them, and this stops them fulfilling their mission on Earth. On these occasions, the higher self calls the spirit within back before they are supposed to return, and their death would be usually a suicide or sudden death. Remember the 99.9.9%; there are times we cannot predict how a human form will react to the high frequencies and us and there are sometimes unforeseen things we cannot foretell. The human becomes chemically imbalanced, depressed and very unwell, and the spirit within high frequency cannot stay in the third dimension host. They then only see one way out to shed them selves of Earth restrictive energy and what they don't understand. This leads to the spirit within returning home to heal and re-plan their next mission. This explanation might be harder to bear if you have lost someone you love to suicide, but you will have greater understanding on your return home to us.

Look at the people who have found great inner strength from great grief, to help others. Examples of this are the people who have set up charities to help find a cure for the disease that took their loved one, or raise money through existing charities. I am sure you are all aware of someone or have seen them on your news programs. Good comes from this grief and pain, and goodness is a wondrous strength you all have within you, but it sometimes takes the loss of loved ones to trigger this. My understanding of this is the third dimension restrictive energy and the limitations placed on you by human nature. Some of humanity shows kindness every day, but few are selfless and use this kindness to help others, some of whom they have never met. These kind, selfless people will never get any benefit for themselves from their actions to help others, but this does not bother them as they are ascending towards the fifth dimension unconditional love energy.

Please remember that part of our learning is the understanding of all physical beings and their behaviour; with this knowledge, we can learn how to help them ascend into a better way of being. We know you ask, why let the young suffer? This is so hard to explain to you, my friends, and as you ascend your world will stop suffering, because only you can change Mother Earth's future path. We do not wish for any being, at any age, to suffer, but the poor state of Mother Earth, the environment, pollutants, fear, and the fast pace you all live at, are causing untold stress to humanity as a whole. When a young child or adult die through sickness, there is a positive way to look at this. Look at their bravery – somehow they know there is more than just the Earth plane, they will live on, and other humans admire their strength as they face adversity. When they pass home, their physical presence is missed and the human mind wonders, what if? What would they have become if they had lived? Part of your ascension is to accept their parting, knowing they live on in the spirit realm, working to change Mother Earth, so the suffering for these sick children and adults can end for future generations.

The cures for some of these illnesses sit at humanity's feet – in nature, while it can still provide. The pollutants of Earth need to be eradicated and by increasing meditation and mind expansion you will gain the power to heal yourselves. You can fuel your world cleanly through the sun, wind and sea; this has always been possible for humanity, and for the last 50 years or more, they have had the technology to do so, but the greed for money has been too much for the ego, and humanity went down the wrong path. We know more and more of you know this now, so try to raise awareness for clean energy in your world.

I cannot stress this enough. I know it does not help the pain we see that many of you have suffered, but believe me, my friends, it is possible to eradicate disease from humanity. Look at the how various tribes of your world are basically disease free, living stress-free, simple lives in remote regions, and look at their diets. I'm sorry if this sits uncomfortably with you, but we know how you can all change, and just little steps by each individual will help this, in the hope that one day, humanity takes the big step needed to save yourselves and your world.

Chapter 5

Spirit within Marceline - *Earth*

My energies had settled well after life within Eliza, the ascension progression consciousness had taken place and I was now established in my next ascension level. My role as healer for returning spirits within was very busy and I felt my leap of conscious awareness was really helping me in the way of being able to look at the incarnated life within as a whole, with my new raised awareness levels.

In between the healing sessions, I was planning my future role as a guide for a physical being on Earth. Some preparation was needed for my role as guide, which included experiencing humanity's wars. This was because I was going to be a future guide during one of your future wars on earth and one would be chosen when it appeared on the timeline. So in preparation, I visited various wars on the Earth's past timelines and after great deliberation, we decided I would benefit from another physical existence. We felt this needed to be in a time of much unrest for Earth, which created war, and this came about in the era of the French revolution in the reign of Napoleon Bonaparte.

This was a very interesting period in your history, watching a portion of humanity change its destiny. I will give a brief outline account of this time period now so you can understand the basis of my next chosen physical joining on Earth. In the 18th century, the monarchy ruled France and was in crisis by the end of the century, one of the reasons being that France had got involved in and helped fund the American Revolution. Another factor was the extravagant spending by King Louis XVI, who ruled from 1754 to 1793, and his predecessor, which had contributed to leaving the country on the brink of bankruptcy. While all of this was happening, the French people were suffering, getting poorer and saw no end to their misery, with the continuous extravagance of the Royal family constantly on show. The Royal family and the rich Lord Nobles, who did not show much concern for their people's welfare, cultivated the unrest leading to the revolution that eventually overturned the French monarchy. While the rich and the church were exempt from paying taxes, the common people were not, and if they didn't pay up, they were imprisoned. I'm sure you feel, as we did, that this was a very unfair society indeed.

When the people heard the royal treasury was empty and there was no money left to help France, the citizens revolted. This was a time of great fear across France, as the rich Nobles were hunted down, and those that had not fled the country were imprisoned and killed. Their beautiful homes were ransacked and often destroyed, but ironically, we did notice that as the things settled down, the democratic and republican high leaders were living in the homes that survived. So the supporters of the revolution were being rewarded and given gifts for their support, while the citizens still starved. Even though these were dark times, a high percentage of the population did not agree with the way the revolution treated people, but they dared not speak out, for fear of also becoming victims. So they went from one regime run by Royals and Nobles, with a large imbalance of wealth, to a regime based on fear – not really the type freedom we wanted to see for humanity.

The French Revolution led to democratic rule and took away the power held by the Catholic Church, and we saw the priests having to escape France to avoid death. To be honest, we did not see much change in this Earth's country after all that dark energy had been released. The French people were still poor as there was no money, and it would take years to rebuild the finances needed to bring help to all the people. The energies lightened to help aid us bring healing, but there were power struggles within the government, and the country was governed for a period as a Republic, until Napoleon Bonaparte declared the French Empire. Following Napoleon's defeat in the Napoleonic Wars, France then went through several further regime changes. These involved being ruled as a monarchy, then briefly as a Second Republic, and then as a Second Empire, until a more lasting French Third Republic was established in 1870. For 10 years, there was a period of far-reaching social and political upheaval in France that lasted from 1789 until 1799, and Napoleon was a key figure in the later expansion of the French Empire. It was ironic that although the French people sought freedom and a democratic society, they ended up being ruled by a dictatorship. Napoleon wanted the France he knew to rule the world, and if you were not a supporter you disappeared, so this was yet another fear-based way of life for the people of France. I'm not sure I will ever fully understand the human ways, you always seem to be reaching for something, to enhance your lives through war and conflict, but the reality is that what you seek is just a touch away – the divine touch of spirit is the only power you need.

You might have wondered what we were all doing while this was going on? Remember each human has guides and we are trying to steer them to a better way of being, dealing with the dark Earth energy of the time. We were placing healing round the ones that were living in fear and tormented in the revolution, and protecting our spirits within.

We often wonder if humanity will ever learn from their mistakes, because even in your modern day there are wars, and innocent lives being taken while two factions fight for supremacy. Your history lies behind you, the message is there for all, and we still have faith that one day humanity will see it. I will be talking more on wars and humanity further in the book, and there is so much of your history on your Earth, in your books and on your Internet, to study and learn from these mistakes. It is key to your ascension that your children learn of humanity's mistakes and do not repeat them. Remember the phrase 'Lest we forget'.

My next blending as spirit within was with Marceline Devore, who was born in France in the winter of 1778 in the small City of St Denis. Located north of Paris, St Denis in your modern day is now a suburb of Paris. Marceline was the only child of Monsieur and Madame Devore. Marceline's father Antoine was a professor of math's and science; he was a very intelligent man, raised in a middle class family who were supporters of change in France, which eventually came in the form of the French revolution.

I thought I would share a brief description of the origins of St Denis in your Earth timeline, as it was of interest to me. Saint Denis was originally a missionary from Italy, and with two others, he set out to convert people to his Christian beliefs. He became a Bishop in Paris in the third century, and was persecuted by the Romans for his belief in Jesus. The non-Christian priests were threatened by his beliefs and Denis was imprisoned by the Roman Governor of the time. Eventually, he was decapitated, and people claimed that the decapitated Bishop picked up his head and walked several miles while preaching a sermon on repentance. Of course this did not happen, but those that had great faith in his teachings exaggerated the story of his death to keep his beliefs alive, and his followers elevated him to be a saint and martyr to his cause. He was then venerated in the Catholic Church as the patron saint of France. After his death, a chapel was raised at the site of his burial by a wealthy follower, which eventually became a beautiful abbey; the area was named St Denis and grew into a small city.

This never ceases to amaze us, how humans can have such a deep-seated belief system that causes harm to others who do not fit into their way of thinking, while others then raise that being into the status of a martyr for all to worship and look up to. We will never harm another and we do have great acceptance and tolerance of all belief systems. We know the divine spark was the original spark for religions, which has lost its way through human ego. There are those who choose power over others and we see often in religions that use god as a cover to create a fear-based faith through brainwashing. The ones with power over their followers gain wealth and self-importance with no thought to others. This can all be seen in the histories of all your countries – the Catholic religion is a prime example. True religion is always in love and making sure others never suffer, as this is the makeup of the true God, our overseers – unconditional love.

Marceline's entrance into the world was not an easy one; her mother Alienor had already lost three children before they took their first breath. Her pregnancy with Marceline was a troubled one and Alienor had to bed rest from four months onwards, as there was a high risk of miscarriage. She went into labour after just eight months, but 24 hours later Marceline arrived safely on a cold January day. I remember the relief in the household following the birth of this long-awaited miracle child. (Those of you who have lost children through miscarriage will understand the joy of the birth of your first surviving child. I mainly felt a sense of achievement and great love; the sex of the child did not matter – what mattered was that all was well with mother and child.)

Her parents' large terrace-style house was on a typical street in St Denis, made from brick and wood, and spread over three stories; all the fronts of the houses faced out straight onto the street with no front gardens, and the roads were cobbled. They had a back garden and because Alienor loved flowers, it was a delight in the warmer months. This was a space where Marceline spent a lot of time with her mother, and I have to admit I enjoyed this too, as it was an uplifting experience being out in nature. In those days, cities were smelly places with sewage, and so to have a small perfumed oasis of your own was very good for you and lifted your spirits.

Marceline's childhood was interesting for me, as she was the only child of two adoring parents, which made her the sole focus of their attention. Her mother had all the household skills and loved embroidery, and she made sure all of this was passed on to Marceline. But she was also educated from a very young age, which I knew was very rare for that time. Being a professor, her father wanted her to understand math's and written language, and felt strongly that all children of both sexes, not just boys, should be fully educated. He also felt they should have the opportunity to study further afield in their late teens and young adulthood. I liked Antoine, as he was a radical thinker for his time, and he was the type of solid foundation France needed. This education led Marceline to love books from a young age. I really enjoyed this and her mind absorbed the knowledge and stories of romance, and her imagination took her on journeys to distant shores. She also liked to write poetry, so I will leave you to have a bit of fun and to translate this poem she wrote:

J'entends des tambours éloignés, le parler de la guerre
J'entends l'air joyeux de l'oiseau chanteur.

Ensuite, il y a eu un silence sur les pensées non entendues
La peur cachée de ce qui se passe.

Un grondement lointain de tonnerre, ou des sabots de chevaux
Des hommes et des femmes couchés par terre.

Ensuite, les tambours éloignés s'arrêtent et la paix monte
J'entends encore l'air joyeux de l'oiseau chanteur.

In 1789, Marceline was 11 years old when the French revolution broke out. I found her poems of this time reflected her fears, and she often heard her parents talking quietly about what was happening in France and Paris. Her father would meet with his friends in his library, and talk of what they thought was to come – they were supporters for change, but were intelligent enough to keep their thoughts in private meetings. They wanted change but more on a spiritual level of wanting an equal society for all; they did not want bloodshed, but knew this would most likely be the way forward. It was an unknown quantity whether or not the people would win this revolution, but once the French king Louis XVI was overturned, it all took on a new momentum, leaving the doors open for change across France. Antoine's first priority was to keep his family safe and fed, and with his network of intellectual scholar friends and others whom they knew, he managed this.

Once the revolution settled, a lot of the war with Europe was so far away, and updates were from distant stories that would filter back through the news streams to Marceline's family. They chose to stay in St Denis, and her father found the education system had improved greatly. Secondary schools were being established in the bigger cities and his skills of learning were sought after, with the curriculum broadening into languages and the sciences. Young children of the age 6-12, both boys and girls, were required to attend schools that were created without charge, so Marceline benefited from this as well. Thanks to her father's teachings she excelled at school, and I saw this did alienate her a little bit from the other young ladies – it was as if it was best not be too bright. However, she was of such an intelligent nature she did not let this bother her, and it was her intelligence as well as her beauty that was to draw her future husband to her.

Marceline first met Marcus Spenard, her future husband, when she was ten years old and he was twenty. He was in the French army and was home on leave, and came with his father to their house for one of their secret meetings where they discussed the problems of France.

I forgot to mention what a beauty Marceline had become; she had strawberry blond hair, green eyes, and had an air about her that was beyond her years. There was no spark of love at this age, but Marcus loved teasing her and answering her questions about the army, and hearing her laugh at his stories. Marcus was born in 1768 in Paris to a non-military family, his father being a learned man like Antoine. He was a very handsome young man with thick jet-black hair, and from a young age he had been drawn to the military life so there was no surprise when he asked to go to a military school, where he excelled. On his home visits, which were rare, he loved to spend time with his father and his scholar friends and listen to their intellect and how they saw the world. To be honest, Marcus was married to his career, so had never looked at marrying anyone. Being a man he had sexual relationships, but away from home in far off lands, with I believe who you would call ladies of the night.

As the years rolled on Marceline and Marcus met only five times, but each time she became more attractive, and she was drawn to Marcus; he was so different from her father's friends, and she loved listening to his tales of army life. He was careful never to divulge the full horrors of war to her, just parts where heroes came forth out of the darkness, and his own successful career. It was in the summer of 1795, when she was 17 years old and he was 27, when the love sparks started to fly. The moment I remember is when they wandered into the garden; it was a perfect summer's day, and the garden was full of perfume from the flowers. I experienced the moment of their first kiss, a wow moment for both of them. From Marcus's point of view, the military career did not seem so important as marriage crossed his mind for the first time. From Marceline's point of view she knew he was the love of her life, two souls meeting across time and entwining with that first kiss.

They married in the spring of 1796, and this was the grandest wedding I had been part of yet on Earth. Lots of Marcus's military friends were there, all their parents, family and friends. They married at the chapel near Marcus's home and the reception was held in Marcus's family home. The house was a delight, a brick structure with wooden paneling inside, and a drawing room with four sets of French windows that went out onto a lawn that swept down to a river's edge. This was a grand house; Marceline had grown to love it and it was to be her future home. Marcus was the only son and heir; his two sisters were married in their own homes by this time and it was natural for the son to inherit in those days. There was not great financial wealth in the family – they had a hard working background, and the house had been passed down to his father from a great uncle. The one thing that stood out to me at the wedding was the high energy and the smiles. There was dancing on the lawn, everybody was so jolly and happy, I felt the suppressive years were being forgotten as they rejoiced this union of two people in love.

Marceline was a little nervous taking up residence in Marcus's parents' home, as when he was away on duty she would be on her own with them, but they were lovely people and made her very welcome. As a honeymoon gift the army gave a leave of absence for a month, and they made the most of it spending every moment together. It was a very hard day when he had to leave to rejoin his regiment; Marceline tried to be brave, but could not conceal her tears, and I could feel her fear of loneliness. Three months after he was gone she discovered she was pregnant, and six months later in early winter 1797, she gave birth to a healthy boy they named Philip. Marcus was not at the birth as he was deployed in Europe, but when the baby was three months old, he came back to his beautiful wife and bonnie son, who looked just like him. Being a mother came easily to Marceline, and she soon discovered she was pregnant again; this time she gave birth to a baby girl they named Jacqueline, in the autumn of 1798. Now, this little girl was miniature version of her mother – it always amazes me how you recreate yourself in your children, in looks and personality, with the human DNA.

Marcus's army life was taking him away for long periods and he was fighting alongside Napoleon in the Napoleonic wars. He missed so much home life, and Marceline was left to deal with his parents' deaths in 1801. They died six months apart from each other – old age had caught up with them – and it was a very sad time in the Spenard household. The only way to contact Marcus was by letter, and I remember well the sadness with which she relayed the news in writing; there was only really one way it could be done, with direct but compassionate language, and brief details of how they died and dates of the burials in the family crypt. As the spirit within, I witnessed Marceline go through short periods of great happiness, then long periods of loneliness, as she wondered if and when her Marcus would come back home safely.

One of the saddest times I can recall is when their daughter Jacqueline died in 1806 at the age of seven. She was a beautiful little girl, reflecting her mother's looks and brains and with the boldness of spirit her father had. I loved to watch her play; she was keen to learn and please her mother and she had a love of nature like her mother had. She had entered this world a strong baby and had had little illness in her short life. One summer's day in her eighth year, she deteriorated with stomach pains, sickness and high fever over a 24-hour period; we knew her appendix had burst, but medicine back then was in its early stages and there was not enough understanding of the human body. The doctor was not sure what it was, and thought it was a nasty stomach bug, but the poison spread through her system and she slipped into an unconscious state. We gave her the healing needed for the transition back to us, and supported the family. I recall the shock and trauma of her death to her mother and brother, as the little spark of light in the house had gone. I admired the strength Marceline found to cope with this without her husband there. Philip was upset but he knew that as the man of house in his father's absence, he had to support his mother the best he could, although he was only 10 years old.

When Jacqueline had passed over, we sent to her mother a white butterfly at the funeral, it landed on the coffin, then on Marceline's arm, and with her joy in the beauty of nature she felt sure this was a sign her daughter was safe in heaven. It was a spiritual moment of recognition in her life, trusting there was something beyond; with the wars and stories of many deaths, she had lost some of her faith and kept asking why so many lives were lost. The loss of a child is the one event that will test all your faiths, as you know, and the butterfly sign gave her hope. From the day of her daughter's funeral, whenever she saw a white butterfly she felt her daughter was near.

Butterflies are such beautiful creatures that reflect the beauty of your world. We love to use them as signs as they signify transformation across many of your cultures on Earth. The butterfly represents the inner spirit that has been released from the physical form. If you have been thinking of a loved one or asking for guidance, and a butterfly lands on you, or near you, know we are close and have heard your prayers.

Later that year Marcus returned home and bought love and happiness back into the home. It had been hard for him to lose a child and not be able to be there to comfort his family. As time was often limited with Marcus's home visits, many matters would be discussed and decisions made about their futures, one of which regarded their son's future education. Marcus wanted him to go to a military school, then on to École Spéciale Impériale Militaire at Saint-Cyr-l'École, situated west of a Paris. It was a boarding school and would mean Philip would be away from home, leaving Marceline on her own with her housekeeper and two dogs. I already knew Philip dreamed of the military life – he idolised his father and loved his army stories on his return from being away.

After Jacqueline's death, Marceline had altered from the young sunny woman she used be; I had witnessed her grief, and missing her husband took a further toll on her, and the sparkle had left her eyes. Now facing this new decision, which she knew was really out her hands, brought a dark cloud down around her. I tried desperately to help her lift this sadness – remember that even though this was her path, we cannot always predict how the human form and inner essence will react. In Marceline's case it was worse than we thought, so we gave healing at times like this to help them move forward.

In Philip's 12th year, 1809, she travelled with Marcus and her son to the school he was to board at. I remember the building, brick with diamond lead windows, set in its own grounds, and Marceline thought it seemed a cold and lonely place. On the other hand, Philip was actually quite excited – he would miss his mother, but since his sister died he had felt lonely and was looking forward to the companionship of others. As planned, at the age of 16, he went on to the École Spéciale Impériale Militaire to train as a young officer. Marceline looked forward to the breaks when Philip would come home and often turned up with a friend for company, or, which was harder on her, Philip stayed away with friends. I saw Marceline settle with herself, her poetry and reading for comfort. She also had a couple of spaniel dogs for company that became her child substitutes, and their love helped break her loneliness.

Marcus had risen to the rank of lieutenant colonel; he was in Napoleon's Imperial Army and was a well-respected strategist and leader. As part of my learning, I would leave Marceline while sleeping and head to the army camps where Marcus was based. I had listened to the many stories he had told his family, but they were played down so as not to show the darkness of those times. The soldiers of the Imperial Army were respected, were treated well by their leaders and, from what I saw, were well-organised. There were various campaigns, which included the seven Coalition Wars. I might be seemingly calmly telling you snippets of this time period, but to be experiencing war as an unseen observer was very hard, although necessary for me to understand humanity's thirst for war and dominance over each other. I knew for this part of my spirit within's journey I would need a lot of protection from my team, to help with what I was to witness.

I really found it hard to understand how a species could tear each other down, taking lives, and witnessing that some humans have no grasp of the consequences of their actions. I tried to understand the mentality 'it's him or me', but at the same time, I started to see that this was the behaviour of a primitive, un-ascended human race. How do I stop this? But then I was reminded it was not achievable as one alone being, but as a collective with other ascension beings, it could be achieved for humanity over time. In these battles, I witnessed fear, great inner strength, callousness, compassion, grief, untold heroism, insanity, cowardice; these are just words used by man and there are so many emotions based round each of those words I selected. Can you imagine how busy humanity's wars keep us, with individual guides giving healing, helping all the spirits within with the transition home. We continuously evaluate humanity, waiting to see if you are learning from all the pain and darkness war causes, and we are always trying to bring a spark of light to humanity, encouraging you to love each other for who you are. I realised at this point that humanity was not learning, and prayed that what I learnt on this physical connection would contribute to any future roles I took to help humanity.

I will not fill these pages with the all the details of the French Revolution, as that is a book in itself, but will enlighten you about Napoleon Bonaparte to help you see how his life was part of Marcus's path in his lifetime. Napoleon was a soldier when the revolution broke out in France, serving as a second lieutenant in the Fére Artillery regiment. He was a supporter of the republican campaign and eventually was made the artillery commander of the republican forces at the siege of Toulon. This ambitious human force became a Brigadier General at 24 years old in 1793. His various positions in the French armies based around Europe and the military campaigns he planned made him very well-known back in France, and in 1799 he returned to France a hero in the eyes of the people.

He saw an opportunity to rule France as a dictatorship, a system that is still seen in parts of your world today. After ten years of constant warfare, France and Britain signed a treaty, after which Napoleon was elevated to Consulate Permanent, and in 1804 he was crowned Emperor of France. By this time war had broken out again between Britain and France and so the bloody battles continued. In 1815, his rule came to an end and he eventually passed away in 1821. Can you imagine what this life was like for the spirit within Napoleon? This was a journey of challenge for both of them, being part of a man of great intellect, vision and drive, and being responsible for many bloody deaths.

We struggle with being part of this human side, and we always hope that human minds will learn from these wars laid down in humanity's history. We hope you realise there is a better way forward with no conflict, but instead, humans choose to study this man, how he created his military campaigns, and use this for further wars. Napoleon was born into the Catholic faith but chose to distance himself from it until on his deathbed, when he took confession with a priest. Looking inside his head, he saw himself as a god that ruled other men and the world. I suppose the words deluded and insane come to mind that are part of your language, but was he? He had a powerful force that drove him forward, never giving up on his vision. Take a look at the war lords of Earth – they all seem to have this energy force to rule over you, and humanity will follow them. To us it looks like brainwashing and ruling out of fear – how else would other humans commit such terrible acts against others unless their minds could not see clearly? I see a weakness in humanity, where you can be easily influenced by others in the third dimension existence, but when you ascend into a clearer way of thinking and see beyond your Earth plane, you will discover the all-knowing way of being that will end these wars.

We remember the question we answered in the book 'Utopia', channelled from us:

Can a soul from another world or dimension merge with our soul while here on earth?

This was a very forward-thinking question from a human. We are aware of cases when this has happened. Our experience of this is it often causes an imbalance in the human body and mind. It can create a leader who will cause harm or destruction, or make a human mentally ill. The reason for this is that the human body energies can only cope with so much. Quite often, the spirit within will step aside from the body if the other energy is stronger, or there can be a switching back and forth in the mind connection, causing a dual personality. We do try to intervene and ask them to leave, and we also have to protect our spirit within while this is in process; this situation also creates great educational learning points in your history and for us.

We have seen examples of this in your history, one of them being Hitler. Like Napoleon, he had unwanted bad energies drawn to him that drove his thirst for power and war. These are spirits that live on the dark side of Earth and choose not to come back home straight away, confused by their physical existence and understanding of transition. We stay connected to them, and work to bring these spirits home to us and heal them back to full pure love energy. When this happens, it affects the higher self, as they cannot progress until their reflection of self blend is completed and healed. As to an negative energy from another realm or dimension entering your human form, yes this can happen, and will cause great imbalance in your energies if not handled properly. This can cause behaviour beyond human comprehension and reasoning of what one human can do to humanity, causing others great harm. This is your Earth's path being allowed to unfold, in the hope humanity will learn from its own history and ascend to the fourth and fifth dimension energies, where the dark energies of the universe can no longer affect you.

After Philip went to boarding school, Marcus only came home from the Napoleon army a couple of times, because he was out in Europe helping with military campaigns. In those days it would take days and weeks to travel anywhere, so when they were out on campaign it was for very long periods of time. On his last visit home I felt Marcus knew it might be his last, as he asked for his son to have a few weeks out of school, and spent a lot of time making sure papers were in order for the home and his will. No words on the subject were spoken, but Marceline was a soldier's wife and had seen many acquaintances lose sons and husbands, so she was aware of the consequences of war. The campaigns were escalating again and there were rumours of Napoleon invading Russia, and thousands of troops were being sent to the front lines. When it was time for Marcus to leave, he held his son and wife for a long time then left without a word and did not look back. Watching this behaviour, I realised the inner strength of determination and bravery it took for him to leave those he loved behind, knowing deep inside he might never return. I don't agree with warfare but having witnessed all this first-hand, I see humans have great strength at times of adversity and when they truly believe their actions to be right, they stick to their convictions.

France invaded Russia in June 1812; there were over 600,000 solders on the front lines. Marcus was leading his troops into battle, as a follow-up group behind the leading French soldiers, which involved long marches as they pushed into Russia. The Cossacks were one step ahead of them, burning the villages and crops before the French troops could restock, trying to starve them out. Marcus's troops were exhausted and starving. One day, they were ambushed and in the fighting, Marcus was struck down with a sword and was injured, the soldiers managed to win the skirmish and escape with their wounded, including Marcus. He had a wound to his upper body and arm, but it was thought that with care, he would recover. He went back to their main camp and was sent home, but died not far from home. One of the wounds was not healing, the travelling did not help his recovery, and his blood got infected on the journey; he slipped into an unconscious state and passed back home to us in the human year 1813, at the age of 45.

It took another week for news of his death to reach Marceline. We knew he had passed and tried to prepare ourselves for the moment of that knock on the door. Marceline opened it to two soldiers; she could tell from the letter they carried and the apologetic look on their faces that Marcus had died. She did not cry out, she stood there numb; they said they had brought back his body so he could be buried in the family crypt. She was grateful for that, so he could be laid to rest with his parents and daughter. After the soldiers left, she sent for their son, and wrote to his sisters and friends; she knew what she had to do and she was mentally prepared for this moment. Even though, when she last saw Marcus, they did not speak of the time he might die, she knew by the way he was behaving he was expecting not to come back for a long time, if at all.

As the spirit within, I could see that Marceline's heart was broken. Her life was empty now; she had her son Philip, but he now had his life as a sixteen-year-old at the start of his military career, dreaming of fighting for his country. She still only had the company of a part-time housekeeper, a few friends and her two devoted old spaniels. I knew her mind was wondering what the future held; she believed in life after death and wondered when she would die and go to heaven to be with her beloved daughter and husband. She could not see any future happiness on her life's path.

In the year 1815 Marceline was taken ill with scarlet fever. This was not always an illness that would kill humans, but she had quite a severe case and with her inner human essence not willing to fight for survival, she gradually slipped away. Her son was called for; a handsome eighteen-year-old with his father's good looks, not even his presence would give her the will to live. She passed one evening with her son and doctor at her side. I remember the scene as I left; she was laid out in white, her long hair brushed, her son kneeling at her side trying to understand why he was now alone in the world, and two dogs that were confused by the whole situation. It broke my heart, but the ones left behind all have a path, and a life on Earth to carry on with. We gave so much healing to them all, and support from us to help them cope with the transition of the loss of Marceline.

Conclusion – My physical life experience with Marceline was over; the main lesson had been to experience humanity at war, from the point of view of Marceline and the soldiers. I see now that to be a wife of any military man takes certain strength, and someone who has to be adaptable and respects their partner. I say this because the military wives endure long periods on their own, making the decisions without the husband's support and sometimes, when the husband returns to the home while on leave, decisions must be questioned and re-examined if they are not agreeable to the returning partner. One of my main observations was that it takes a special relationship to withstand this.

There is no doubt that humanity alone creates the wars on Earth, although we have no wish for there to be any conflict for humanity – please refer to the third, fourth and fifth dimension explanation. We chose to select the physical union with a being that would be a soldier purely to learn from their behaviour and those around them. Back over ancient times and leading up to modern day, warfare has involved a lot of manpower to give the strength to win battles. By the time of the Second World War, a high level of manpower was still required, with the aid of artillery, air and sea support. Your modern day warfare has developed now to need fewer human soldiers and more hi-tech weaponry to show your power over your adversaries.

I witnessed the male population in Napoleon's time wanting to fight for their country and for what they believed in. The flip side of the coin is that we see the thirst for war has come from indoctrination from the leaders of this time and even then, the newspapers influenced humanity's thoughts too. I witnessed lots of soldiers deaths on a massive scale, but in amongst all of this there was comradeship, fear, dread, prayer, celebration, sadness, loneliness, a clarity of life and acceptance of the inevitable death. I saw this test men and women's faith in their religions and acceptance of an afterlife.

There are various reasons for wars on Earth, and it always amazes me when we see faith and religion being used as the excuse for war – and I ask myself often: when will humanity realise there is not one god but the overseers? Napoleon saw himself as a god, the ruler of France, Europe and far beyond. I felt there was a slight insanity about him but as I have already said, there was also a great inner strength, determination and faith in his own self. These are the reasons that humans followed him, because his energy was quite strong and forceful, although I would add, in a dark way.

My time connected as spirit within Marceline was again not for many of your Earth years, but she experienced a lot of emotion for a short lifespan. These emotions included a mixture of love, trust, motherhood, acceptance, loss of a child and loneliness. I saw what humanity could do to each other and how your energies can alter, seeing your human essence fade, causing unhappiness and feelings of loss, and thoughts like 'what is life all about?' and 'why are we here?' I can promise you that when you to learn to live in love and light, showing kindness and support to all around you, the spirit within will no longer witness these feelings. Humans will live in joy and acceptance of each other, causing no harm. Can you imagine this, my friends, what a wonderful place Mother Earth would be?

I have to admit I did feel a difference in my own energies as spirit within this time, because I had stepped up a level in my ascension and was experiencing everything with more clarity. There was less emotion and a more matter of fact outlook, if that makes sense to you. I was starting to understand the human race and seeing the bigger picture of what life could be for them if only they could change. My love for you all is what keeps bringing me back to Earth, so I can bring something new back to the knowledge pot of learning, information that will help us ascend humanity to where you need to be. I see goodness in you all; you are all unique individuals, and you can live as one and retain this individual uniqueness, as we do too.

Chapter 6

Spirit within Isliquine - *Castrolian*

In the time between my physical existences on Earth I had been listening to other beings and the places they visited while carrying out my role as a healer. There was one particular planet I was drawn to called Castrolian, at around 1830 on your timeline on Earth.

To describe where this planet is means taking you far, far away from your solar system, my friends, millions of light years as you call the distance in space. Imagine the universe is round; this solar system would be on the far side of the circle. It is a planet that orbits a sun which is larger than Earth's; Castrolian is one of twelve main large planets within that solar system orbiting around their sun. The planet that contains life we can connect with is smaller than Earth and orbits around a larger planet. I think this larger planet bears the closest resemblance to your planet Saturn in its appearance, and there are also a couple of moons that go round this planet too. Castrolian has some similarities to Earth; it has a liquid substance that helps to sustain life, as water does on Earth, but the make-up of the liquid is chemically different and is a life source produced from inside the planet. The planet has plant life, animals and physical energy beings inhabiting it. Its history of existence is all very similar to Earth's timeline and solar system.

The inhabitants of Castrolian are part of a civilisation of beings that are very ethereal in nature. Think of the elemental beings and fairies of your world that live in the elemental kingdom veiled from you; these beings are similar in their way of existing. They protect their planet and live in what you would understand as a loving, kind way to each other. They do not hurt each other and there is no hate or anger amongst them, but like humans, they do have a lot of emotions – for example they suffer pain and loss when one of their own dies or is physically hurt. I would say that compared to the beings on Earth, they have ascended beyond the fourth dimension and are now ascending into the fifth dimension way of thinking and being.

They now have telepathic powers and spoken language for communication, with the dialects varying slightly around the planet. But as time progresses, the spoken language is becoming less important as the telepathic mind expands. With entering the fifth energy frequency, their consciousness is expanding to aid this telepathic progress. They do not have wars, and they don't segregate themselves as Earth does into different races and religions. They live in communities around their planet assisting and helping each other, and this has assured their survival. As you know, planet Earth has its hot and cold climates, but because of the way this planet is situated within its solar system, enjoying the protection of a larger planet, they do not experience the same extremes of climate.

They do have a seasonal existence and their days and nights are shorter than yours, but they do not live by time restricting their lives – they have ascended beyond that. There was a time when their civilisation was more focused on time-keeping, but they have now grown out of the third dimension limited way of thinking and now they see everything differently. As you can imagine, the ascension of this planet has been very interesting to us and I would say these beings never had the destructive tendency your humanity has, to hurt each other and Mother Earth. So when we join with them it's a more relaxing experience for us, my friends; we do experience a physical existence, but it is advanced to where we hope humanity will be in one to two hundred or so of your Earth years. This gives us hope for you all as we learn from this planet Castrolian.

The being I became part of as spirit within was of female gender; she was a highly ascended young being, a very beautiful creature called Isliquine, which means Noble One in their language. I would say the nearest comparison between their looks and yours are your Earth illustrations of fairies with pixie features, but they have smaller mouths and ears. They have mainly silver blond hair and smooth skin which is pale lilac in colour. Their planet has a lighter gravity and they do breathe, but their air is thinner and they have learnt to adapt and live off the energy sources of their planet. Their form resembles humans with limbs and a similar physical make-up, but if you saw them today, you would see a glow around them radiating out. As you know, humans have energy auras that some of you are lucky enough to see; the strong energy field around each Castrolian would be visible to all humans! They have learnt to tap into their planet energy source, to aid their physical energy existence. They nourish themselves and fuel their energy levels with what I would best describe to you as a vegetable diet, along with the energy source connection from their planet. The plant life creates an energy as well as a source for the air they breathe, and it's this combination that helps them survive and exist. They have never eaten the creatures of their world, even in their primitive past, as they have always respected and worshipped the nature of their planet.

There is no threat to their planet like pollution or war weapons as you face on Earth, my friends, it is all very stable on Castrolian. They have clean energy and their power source for heat and lighting is produced from their natural resources such as their sun and wind power. This might be hard for you to imagine, but they do not know of the use of fire for heat – which was, of course, the spark for starting a lot of Earth's development. Their planet also does not suffer extreme hot or cold temperatures; it stays at a fairly even temperature that sustains them. Because of how they are developed and the deep-rooted respect for what the planet provides, they have always respected Castrolian and never harmed their life source, taking only what they need for survival, with thanks to their planet. Their spiritual way of living reminds us of your Earth's Native American Indians and other ancient tribes.

Through their ascension, the Castrolians have telepathically connected to us and to the universal knowledge pot, and have decided as a collective that there are certain things they do not want to introduce into their world. This is because it would threaten their peaceful existence; with their great foresight and knowing, it is quite an amazing place to be part of. Even for us, it is quite humbling to be part of these physical beings, as they do not have religion and do not worship a god. Instead, they worship their planet and they do this by showing it respect; it is an amazing experience for us to witness, as this is what we want for all of you. I would also say to you, my friends, that there was a time when they were not aware we were with them as spirit within, although they have always had a belief of living beyond their existence, and feel their loved ones' energies after they have passed. They thought what they were feeling was because they were so attuned to their planet and her energies.

The thing to remember is the high ascension beings that help you don't need to be acknowledged and worshipped. We are happy to be part of their existence, guiding them towards the fifth dimension state as we do with you and other beings, through telepathic suggestion and healing when needed. The time did arrive when they saw us for what we are, because they became purer in thought and had greater understanding of themselves, the spirit realm and the universe as a whole. They are a great asset to the universal galactic group of highly ascended beings whose role is to guide and help other beings towards the love and light way of being. Remember, their story and knowledge is in the universal knowledge pot for others to learn from, and I wait for the day when you can connect to this wonderful place and see for yourselves their entire story.

I can use the phrase 'great knowing' quite a lot, so I thought I would explain it to you. It is when your mind and all your senses have ascended in the fourth and fifth dimension way of thinking. How can I explain this? Imagine you are standing in a garden and you observe a bee. As you are in your third dimension way of thinking you would see the bee, hear the buzz of its wings and then be distracted by other things very quickly, including your thoughts. When you have ascended in mind and body you would be able to choose to see the bee suspended in the moment, as if you were seeing it in slow motion, and you would be able observe its movements, feelings and language. While doing this, you would still be aware of the normal world around you and be able to see beyond that moment as well. I know this is hard to imagine, but it is a wonderful way to exist.

This power comes from ascension and clearing of the mind to bring clarity of what could be. Have any of you ever meditated and noticed the ticking of a clock you have never noticed before while in the third dimension busy energy world? This is because when you meditate, you elevate your senses and when the mind is focused, the clarity of what's all around changes, as if you are suspended in the now moment. Where you are in your own space slows, your mind reaches the fourth dimension energy level, although you are still in the third dimension energy plane of your world. So you see, if you all reach this type of understanding of how your third dimension world would shift to the fourth dimension higher energy grid, your minds as a collective would connect and raise your Earth energies towards the love and the light. Remember, we would be with you all the way, helping with the energies and adjusting them to help you ascend.

My entrance into their world was so different to my Earth experiences, as they produce their young in very different way to yours, which I'll try to explain the best I can. They carry the seed of life within each gender, and when they meet the mate of their choice, they then choose the time to have their young. The female of their species releases an egg cocooned in a transparent hard shell, which comes from an organ like a small gill on the side of her body; the male then releases from his gill fertilisation pods that sprinkle over the shell of the egg. The shell is then safely placed in an natural environment incubator connected to the planet's life source. Tentacles form from the shell to link to the planet source of life force energy and as it does, the outer shell turns a light purple. The young being is nourished by this planet energy source, helping the young Castrolian being to grow, developing its gender, individual essence and character while cocooned in its own shell.

The time of development is equivalent to Earth's seven months. The shell grows as the youngling develops when the being is ready to be born, the cocoon shell changes colour to a dark purple and it cracks open. The young Castrolian being is lifted out and separated from its energy source, which has been connected to the gill on the right hand side of their body. The young being then starts its life with its family group, very much the same as humanity. They have a longer life compared to the average human, but this has mainly come about from their ascension, self-healing and healthy life styles. From their side gill they have silvery tentacles that connect to certain plant sources that provide the energy source to recharge. The best way to describe this is that they connect to huge tree-like plants that grows around their planet. If you could see these huge plants, you would see a glow of purple energy that runs through them like blood, and this is what the Castrolians link into. The trees produce vines that reach wherever they are needed. This is how the young feed too; they do not feed from their mother and then when they mature, they can also consume plant matter for the other nutrients they need.

While I was spirit within the cocooned shell, it was like being connected to the heart of the planet, I felt aware of her history and the love she has for her off-spring, the Castrolians, because this planet is a living entity in her own right. (Remember the elementals on earth and how they look after Mother Earth; your earth is also a living entity radiating her feelings and light out into the universe.) It was quieter, because in the human womb we are a lot more aware of voice noise, the tensions of the human's body, and those around us. But my experience within Isliquine was so peaceful and tranquil - actually reflecting the life that was to come.

Her mother Josteline and her father Twyntal came from a community on the planet called Jestdol. Their communities were beautiful and I found their homes rather beautiful too, as they are carved from a crystal substance the planet provides for them to create upright, layered structures that sparkle like mirrors, reflecting the beautiful world around them.

I bet by now you have lots of questions you want to ask me about Castrolian, so I'll try to give you some basic information on how they live:

The males and females are similar in appearance, but the females are more delicate in features and slightly smaller than the males. They have pale lilac skins and fine silver blond hair. Just above their brow is a section of skin over their bone structure that protrudes out and then recedes back, which is the start of their hairline. The hair is straight and usually long for both sexes. They have the equivalent of lungs and heart and the liquid in their veins has a translucent glow to it, like you see with fluorescent glow on Earth. They have no kidneys or liver, but they have a food filtration system in their body that does all this for them. They have three very long, slim fingers and a thumb equivalent, and feet with four toes. They do not have body hair apart from on their head, mainly due to the constant climate they have adapted to. I would say that if you saw a group of them you would think they were all very similar in appearance. But as you adjusted to their world and got to know them, you would understand the difference, that they each have individual personalities and uniqueness about them. Their general life span is longer than yours; I would say the equivalent of 90 to 150 years of Earth time. The planet population is a lot smaller than Earth and most Castrolians will mate for life and have one or two children. They are drawn to their partner by an inner connection, quite often bonding when young. They hold a matching ceremony with their whole community present when the time is right for them to live together. At these ceremonies they play music through long crystal pipes and they dance too; believe me, this is beautiful to hear and see.

They wear garments to cover up their form, which are mainly practical clothes and made from a plant that they process and weave into fabric. The nearest texture to this on your world would be your silk, but theirs has a tougher fibre. They also like to decorate their non-working clothes with gems and crystals, which are easily found on the planets surface, especially near the flowing energy sources. On special occasions, they also use their world's flora to decorate their hair and homes, appreciating the beauty of their nature.

Their lighting comes from a crystal that absorbs the sun's energy and reflects out the light when it's dark, rather like your solar light but without the electrical components. I think what I love about this planet is how it provides, through natural sources working in harmony with the Castrolians. They also have another crystal stone that gives out heat absorbed from the planet's energies and sun, which is used for a mixture of warmth and cooking.

If you've asked this question in your heads, the Castrolians do have to go to the toilet like humans, but only have one body exit for this, and the compost system in their homes takes it back to their planet to be recycled. Remember, there are no pollutants on this planet; they have managed to keep it very pure with their respect for their home. They also do not need to wash every day as you do, as their bodies self-cleanse; the human body is capable of this too, if allowed to develop. It is your mind that rejects your smell – the Castrolians have odour too, but it does not repel them from each other.

Communication is through spoken language, telepathic means, technology and travel. Their telepathic skills are very enhanced now and are overriding the spoken language. Their main source of travel is flight, for which they use a clean, crystal-based gravity energy source with rechargeable properties. Their flight machines do not have wings – they use a power that raises them from the ground and propels them to their destination. They also have boat crafts as they enjoy their equivalent of a water source on their planet, and these crafts hover across the flat energy lakes as well as the flat parts of land. The machines are made from a single mineral source that can be manipulated to their needs. Extraction of this is closely monitored and comes from one part of their planet.

They sleep in resting areas in their homes mainly to rest their minds; during sleep, the tentacles from their gills plug into their planet's source of energy. This is a vine-like growth that comes from a special plant already described; the vines appear to have pulsating veins, which contain the energy from the planet source.

The Planet is alive, full of energy and recorded in time; deep-set into its crystal cores is the history of the Castrolians and their teachings. Through time, the physical beings of the planet connected to this source for life and education. The knowledge that is held in the planet's crystal cores is transferred to the energy source for the Castrolians to absorb deep into their minds. This is a bit like transferring a planet DNA pattern of thought, and they have also learnt to telepathically transfer knowledge and images into crystals. They use shafts of crystal about eighteen inches long and one inch across; they are hexagonal and are placed into their technology. The technology can then reflect this information in imagery around the Castrolian that is using it, or it can connect to their thought patterns. Due to their ascension level, they can also now take themselves into the situation or the subject, and experience it as if they are part of it, a bit like your virtual reality experience on Earth.

Do you know that your Mother Earth also has amazing crystals in her layers, and crystal caves that also hold her knowledge? Aliens that have visited your planet have left information and footprints of their existence in the crystals for humanity to discover one day. When you have ascended into a more telepathic way of being and can clear your minds, you will be able to hold these crystals to obtain the information you need to aid humanity. We will guide you to these crystals when the time is right for you to receive this knowledge.

As for illness, Castrolians do have types of bacteria on their planet that can cause them to feel off-colour, but they use mind-based healing and natural remedies to heal themselves now. It is mostly old age that takes them from their families; similar to you, their bodies wear out but they do live longer than they used to and we see this increasing in their future timeline.

As to the rulers of Castrolian, they have their overseers for each populated area; there are six in total around the planet. For example, Jestdol has twelve elders who oversee the community; they are elected for their experience to ensure their values are maintained, and especially that they are taught to the young and fully explained. Remember the access to the Universe knowledge pot; this shows them new technologies and other places, but they know with their clarity of thinking that they take just what serves them all for the best – for example, their method of flight was an idea from this pot. They also know not to invite less ascended beings to visit their planet, or take on new technologies they don't understand or that will not serve the greater good, as this would destabilise their way of life. So they protect themselves, and they are now ascended to this early fifth dimension energy level, bringing unity and love, with no greed or harm to others.

We must not forget their nature and animal kingdom. The most similar animals to yours are like your horses, but taller with longer necks, running in herds and very spiritual. There are creatures very like the Earth cat family, as well as flying creatures that live off the nectar of plants, and creatures that burrow in the ground. As on Earth there are predators amongst Castrolians creatures that live off each other as well as off vegetation and the planet energy source. There is a natural order to things in their animal kingdom, which if uninterrupted helps keep the creatures' populations under control. Their habitats remain untouched and the planet's nature is allowed to stay balanced as the Castrolians respect her and understand that for their survival, it is important the planet is unpolluted. The animals live in harmony with the Castrolians in unity, and connected to the planet source of energy; through their evolution, all of these beautiful beings understand this.

Now back to my time as spirit within Isliquine. As I have already said, the experience of conception and development of the young Castrolian being was so different to Earth's. The development period of the pod is equivalent to seven months' Earth time and the chemical change on the outside of the pod darkens to a deep purple, which is a sign that all is ready for the little being to come into the world. A natural crack appears around the pod and falls away, and the new life emerges with their parents' assistance. The egg pods are placed in their homes for the development and growth period, connected to the plant life source. The pods are always watched over with excitement and love. I experienced a very strong protective bond full of unconditional love for this young Castrolian being from her mother and father. One of the first things that hit home to me was how strong the family unit was, all living very near to each other and with their long lifespan, the family support is quite constant.

For comparison, I witnessed these strong family units and from this I knew how vital it is for the mental and physical health that a strong family unit full of love is what feeds the human essence and spirit within. The difference between Earth and Castrolian is that every family unit on Castrolian has this wonderful bond, key to their thriving way of existence. Sadly on Earth, it is through the third dimension energy causing fears, human ego leading you down the wrong paths of choice, lack of morals, addiction, disdain for and misunderstanding of others – the list goes on – that causes weak family units. The reason I raise this is because Earthlings and Castrolians are similar, and for them to thrive and ascend the family unit is key. The Castrolian history line shows me a time when they were not so considerate of each other, but they have ascended into the way of thinking that unity provides life for all and everyone is as important as everyone else. Not all beings in the universe live in family units and some survive in different ways, but you two are similar in our view, that's why we like to visit you both for comparisons and learn from one to help the other.

Isliquine was the only child of Josteline and Twyntal. She brought completion to their relationship and became one of their main focuses in life, enjoying watching her grow and develop in their beautiful world. Her parents' role in their community was overseeing the harvest of plant food and protection of the ecosystem on their lands, always making sure a balance was maintained in what they needed and what was harvested for consumption. They did not have to farm as the planet provided the food sources in abundance in natural settings, which would then be harvested. The foods would be distributed fairly to all, which was a combination of fruits and vegetables. I'll try to explain the vegetation to you as it is different, it's not green like earth, more various shades of grey-blue, hints of purple, very tall, with vines carrying the energy flow of life. The plants producing the food have what you would think of as exotic-looking flowers, and the seedpods can float spiralling in the air. The pods are guided by the planet energy, distributing themselves to where they are needed, and the planet energy source is then their food; as their roots take hold, they give life.

What I really enjoyed about being spirit within Isliquine was that there was no fear. By this, I mean the deep-seated fear I experienced on Earth, of surviving from day-to day the fear of being hurt by others, who might take what was theirs. This fear that humans give off around a child is absorbed into your energy fields and I picked up on this – it's a fear we want to lift from your planet.

The only fear, (if you can even call it that) I felt with this young being on Castrolian would be while playing, learning the boundaries in their world of nature, the dos and don'ts of day-to-day life. As with all Castrolian's, the outside was their playground, and they were even taught some of their lessons in outside spaces, which helped inspire them. Isliquine was a very inquisitive child who loved exploring and climbing the plant life around their community. She had a group of friends that kept all their parents on their toes and brought laughter to all. She also loved her lessons; they did not have paper or books, but used Crystal technology that recorded their history. They had a device in which they could place these crystal tubes, which would project the knowledge needed around them and also link to their thoughts. Their schooling was not every day – perhaps one daylight cycle a week – as they had no exams, colleges or universities as you know on Earth. They learnt about their planet, their history, and about their ascension, and how they have reached the point they are at now. They also learnt how to look to the future, and what they need to do to build on this understanding and new clarity of mind. They learn the balance of keeping their planet safe, but carry on ascending at the same time. When they are older, the last stage of this education is on the universal knowledge pot, but they are only allowed to access this when they show mature clarity of mind.

I must point out here that you can only access the knowledge pot if you are pure of heart and mind, which is why it's only open to highly ascended beings; we monitor this with the chosen affiliated ascended beings we work with. When we feel a planet, realm or dimension is ready to receive such knowledge we then reveal ourselves to them. As you can imagine, this was an amazing event on Castrolian's timeline. We knew and trusted that they would only take what they needed to build a better world for themselves, with all minds in love and light. Only the older Castrolians of great understanding have this high access, and they monitor who may access it on their planet. It's certainly not for the very young; we wait until their minds have matured to the understanding level needed for this, which will happen in the same way for humanity one day.

As I watched Isliquine grow up, her days were filled with laughter and life lessons, always under the watchful eyes and minds of her parents and elders in the family unit. I say minds, as with their telepathic abilities she was always just a thought away. She would also follow her parents around on their day-to-day duties of overseeing the food gathering and the monitoring of the lands of Jestdol. I observed that the children quite often followed their parents into their adult roles, but Isliquine was very interested in teaching and being an overseer of their knowledge. The Castrolians were a very bright people, but Isliquine was more intelligent than most. We found that this increased intelligence was being seen more often in their young, as their expanding telepathic minds created a greater thirst for knowledge. Key to being a teacher when her cycles of years were ready was having the knowledge, knowing and passion to teach, at the same time protecting Castrolian and its way of life to ensure their future survival.

I explained earlier that the children of this world do not have schools or further education. They are taught in various ways. They receive information from their connection to the planet, through their connection when they link to their planet energy while in their birth pod, and as they develop and recharge through life. This learning consists of memories of the planet's history, and their cellular level for self-healing and understanding of the world around them. Next, their parents and elders teach them the day-to-day values of life and how their community lives and works. Then they have the crystals that hold information about the planet's history, any technology they have, and new developments. They have a written language, but since their telepathic abilities have enhanced it is not used much anymore.

What I have not mentioned yet is their art and music. The art is very beautiful, using the various colour pigments of their plant life and soils. The art portrays their history, stories of past times and their planet. Now their music is very beautiful, and made with an instrument similar to the flutes you have on Earth, but made from a crystal. They blow into the instrument, which has specially positioned holes to create the notes, and the melodies are enchanting, capturing the essence of these beautiful beings. They also have a form of singing, more pitches of sound set in a rhythm of harmony; it is difficult for me to explain to you all, as our highly-ascended senses cope with this, but your third dimension senses would hear it all differently.

Each community on Castrolian has access to all these teachings and knowledge in their homes, as well as in a community space that I suppose you would know as a library. A teacher on Castrolian visits the homes making sure the right knowledge is being accessed, and arranging teaching times at their central gathering place of knowledge. As mentioned before, there are also teachings in the open air about the planet, art and music. The teachers have a responsibility to keep adding knowledge as it develops on the planet.

As Isliquine grew up it was obvious her interest was not with her parents' role in the community. By her fifteenth life cycle it was clear that teaching was her path, and the elders of her community ensured she had direction from the teachers among them. She was so delighted by this experience and spent many hours studying, so she excelled in this role among her community, as she wanted to achieve the best for all. It was wonderful to see Isliquine growing up confident about her future with no fears, and all the support and love she needed to achieve the future goals she had set herself.

Now while I am mentioning love, Castrolians bond for life, and love is a strong force they feel for each other when the chemistry is right between two of their kind. Isliquine had grown up with a neighbour's son Tryanto, who was a life cycle older, and their families were very close as both sets of parents had also grown up together. Tryanto was someone she could confide in; he always supported her in her escapades while they were young, and with what she chose to be when she was older, and he liked her just as she was. Tryanto was interested in forms of travel and flying, so he was looking at becoming the equivalent of an engineer on Earth, looking after the flying machines in their community and eventually flying them. His father had had some involvement in the designing of the modern versions of these machines, so this had helped fuel Tryanto's interest. Isliquine and Tryanto were so comfortable with each other they had not realised the love they felt for each other, but I remember the day well when they discovered it.

It was in Isliquine's eighteenth-year cycle when they were both just wandering through the beautiful landscape towards a lake; they loved this space as the lake reflected the planet nearby and the stars. The foliage and flowers were wonderful and they loved watching the creatures flying and skimming across the energy of the life-source lake. Their favourite was a creature similar to your butterflies but a lot larger, with layered wings that rippled as they flew, their unique colours shimmering in the light. They both sat next to each other just watching their world, then Tryanto suddenly turned and faced Isliquine and took her in his arms. The way Castrolians bond physically is not through kissing and sexual organs as you know, but by touching the raised part of their foreheads. When this happens and the sexual chemistry is right, there is an elevated touch of minds and body that would be an equivalent to an Earth being's orgasm. This was their moment of life bonding, and it was a beautiful experience for me to see and feel. When they revealed this to their parents, everyone was very happy. They held a matching ceremony to celebrate their bonding with their family and community. The bonding would then trigger in them both the life seeds for their young. Bonding can take place from their seventeenth cycle onwards, as their bodies are not ready before that. If for some reason they lose their partner through death when younger – which is rare – they can re-bond with another partner if the chemistry is right for them to do so.

From the moment of their bonding, they wished to be together, so the family all helped to build them their first home in their community, set within their family groups. Isliquine carried on with her studies for teaching and Tryanto was fulfilling his passion for building flying machines – like his father, he had a flair for design. At his home, he had a space to tinker with new ideas and designs; in fact quite often, Isliquine had to drag him away from his work to enjoy the outdoors they so needed to sustain their Castrolian essence in life.

It was wonderful to see these two Castrolians live their happy, fear-free lives and as they grew older they were very respected in their community. The elders that oversaw their community saw qualities in Isliquine that suggested she would be an elder herself one day, and her intelligence and passion for her world created the unique balance they sought to continue a peaceful, united existence.

When Isliquine reached her Thirtieth year cycle, she and Tryanto decided it would be a good time to have a child. Now there was some preparation for this, as they needed to make sure they had the right space in their home and the life-source vine for the seedpod of life to connect to. When this was all ready, they would then choose their moment to come together. It was a repeat of the bonding ritual I have already described, but with an elevated intent of reproducing their young. They came together and bonded and as this happened the gill released tentacles that connected to each other; within this process, the seed of life cocooned in a shell pod was released from Isliquine with the tentacles holding it in place, then Tryanto released from his gill small seed pods of life that attached to Isliquine's seed pod of life, and they then bonded to each other. When it was over they removed the cocooned seedpod of life and placed it in the area created for its development. Over a few cycles of days the pod grew connecting tentacles to the planet's vine life-source, and the incubation period began. Now like all life-forms, there are occasions when this process can fail, and then there is sadness, as they already have a bond with the tiny forming being. But as with you on Earth, Castrolians give it a space of time and healing before they try again.

I am pleased to say, though, that this was a success for them and they had a son who they named Lishion, meaning loved one. It was lovely to have the privilege of witnessing the creation of their son and the love all the family had for him. The family bond was so strong that they all had a say and a hand in his upbringing. This young Castrolian being inherited his mother's intelligence, passion for his planet and his dad's creativity; because of this, he was destined to be a leader amongst his community as well.

They chose only to have the one child, as their careers were very busy and key to the development of their planet. When Isliquine reached her 50-year cycle she was a senior teacher in her community, and had access with the elders to the knowledge pot from the high ascension beings helping them. She had by this stage telepathically connected with them and seen them in communications through their expanding technology. In her 58th year cycle she became an elder of her community. This was a wonderful day to observe and all were so proud and happy for her to be one of their overseers. She continued in this role to her 81st cycle when her health declined a little, and she felt she could no longer fulfil her role as she wished. I saw that she was very happy to retire and enjoy life with her extended family and granddaughter Pesdican. In her 90th year cycle, she became very weak and the healers of their world could not help her anymore, as old age was taking over. One day, she asked her son and Tryanto to carry her to the lake where Tryanto and she had first bonded, and she lay there in Tryanto's arms and quietly passed away.

As I left her body, I stayed for a while to observe them, Tryanto held her tight and eventually their son had to separate them so he could carry her home for all to mourn her. She was laid out in their home so everyone could pay their respects, then a couple of days later she was taken to her chosen resting place by the lake and buried in the planet's soil, so she could return to the source of their creation. The grave was marked with a crystal stone that holds her life's achievements for all to observe in the future.

Conclusion - This is the easiest conclusion for me as I felt I had been on a spiritual holiday. I was so pleased I had experienced this physical existence with these wonderful beings. Many, many cycles of their planets ago they were a civilisation in a third dimension energy existence, as Earth is now. But they had not developed the fear and hate humanity has for each other. The Castrolians were always loyal to their planet and the life force it gave them, and no matter how primitive they were they always understood this. One of the reasons for the way they developed was their need of the planet's life energy source for birth and life. The planet has a built-in intelligence that keeps the Castrolians in this way of thinking.

The Castrolians' ascension into the fourth dimension energy was easier than Earth's, as they had already attended to and respected their planet. They adapted to a loving existence in unity with all Castrolians, ensuring their planet's survival and each other's. It was at this point we could get very excited about this planet, and worked towards the day we could reveal all to them. As we have said before, there are other ascension beings that help us, and their knowledge and journeys to high ascension sit within the universal knowledge pot. I should mention we have knowledge of all worlds, realms and dimensions, even those that have destroyed themselves, or are struggling to ascend. The ascending beings like the Castrolians have access to the knowledge of those helping their planet and can then choose what could benefit them. This is to ensure peace and security amongst the ascension beings, as they could put their way of being at risk. We have to make sure this knowledge is kept hidden from beings that would abuse their power and technology by using it as a power over to gain dominance, with the intent of harm to others. We patiently wait until we know they are ready and can be trusted with the enormous enlightenment that it brings.

I also felt this physical existence as spirit within had given me the nudge I needed to keep the faith for Earth and humanity. I saw in the Castrolians some of the good human traits I had witnessed, like love, faith, commitment, support and kindness. These are things I think we can forget you all have within you, as we have spent so long trying to get you out of the fear and anger energy around Earth at the moment. Even we need to regroup and remind ourselves why we do what we do, and keep our energies up in the love and light to help humanity.

Chapter 7

A guide to Harry - *Earth*

Wow – the time had come for me to be a guide to a incarnated soul in a physical being and I was very excited. I had been working hard with my development, and my physical spirit within experiences had given me a good grounding for being a guide to a physical being.

First of all I thought I would re-cap about guides and their purpose. Since we started being the spirit within a physical being, we knew we would need support from our fellow ascension friends while on this journey, and we felt it should come from the experienced incarnation teams. The main purposes of guides are to give advice, guidance and healing to the spirit within and physical being while on the incarnated physical journey. The guide is also responsible for monitoring their journey and collecting information that will then help aid the healing process when they return home.

It was decided a long time ago that every physical being we incarnated into would have a guide that would accompany the spirit within while in a physical form from birth to death. Some of you call this guide a Gatekeeper – the main guide that guides your entry to this life and return back home. These Gatekeeper guides have wide-ranging experience, and will have undertaken various lives as spirit within, giving them a deep understanding of any problems that might arise, alongside the deep wisdom they have gained from their life experiences. There are also two additional guides there to support the main guide; their role is to run errands back to the spirit realm, source information as needed, and give healing. Depending on their experience, they may also use their own learning as guidance to aid the spirit within. Other guides will join you on your journey, dictated by major factors on your path when there are important changes in your life – motherhood, education, health and spiritual development are just a few examples. So you have the same three guides with you all the time, and others coming and going as needed.

A lot of humanity will be unaware of changing guides, but those that have opened to the higher energies and have an understanding of their own energies will sense when this happens. As one guide leaves and another joins you, it causes an energy dip and the new guide has to adjust to your energy field before they can work with you properly, and this can take a few of your Earth days to happen. As well as guides, you will have at least two guardian angels; these are from the high divine overseer dimensions in the higher ascended levels; they have not had a physical spirit within experience so their energy is purer and on a higher frequency. They will be with you to watch over you, offer protection and give healing when called upon by you and us. You are aware of some of the highly ranked guardian angels such as Archangel Michael, but there are thousands more all serving humanity and other worlds as well as our own.

I would also like to make you aware that your guides would be made up of various high-ascended star beings. There are many species that have an alliance with Earth to help us, over seen by the overseers. There is a council called the Intergalactic Council that has members from every species that are involved in the incarnation program. We often have collective meetings about how to help Earth, where we swap information and plan our next step forward to help aid your evolution on the ladder of ascension.

I must add here that when we have completed our time as a guide, we don't need the healing process as the spirit within does after being connected to the physical form. This is because the spirits within have been touched on a deeper level – in a way, hot-wired more to the physical being. Every guide has a debriefing period where we discuss the journey as we saw it, what we could contribute, what we observed and what we learnt to bring back to the spirit realm knowledge pot. This debriefing is with all the guides, ascension beings and Archangels that were attached to the physical being we were looking after, as well as their spirit within higher self form.

I was honored to be chosen to be one of the two support guides to Harry Jones, born in London's East End in June of 1929. Do remember when I was telling you about the lessons I planned to learn with Marceline in Napoleon's time? Some of these centered on war, and my learning was leading to this experience as a guide with Harry.

I will now tell you about this young being's experiences in the Second World War on your Earth.

Harry was the youngest sibling born into a family of seven children. My time as guide started from his first breath and this was such a different experience for me. I could see him as a physical energy being and I could see the pure light of his spirit within, shining bright. At this early stage I was more an observer, and was still carrying on with my normal life. When I was needed I received a telepathic thought from his spirit within or gatekeeper guide and I would be there to help, guide and observe. The ascension advancement I mentioned earlier now lets me be in more than one place at a time, through thought. The best way I can explain this is that I can project part of myself to where I am needed, gather the information and help, and then return to myself in my physical form, and become whole. This has become a natural way of being to us and we have the ability to stand on the edge of the third dimension energy matrix of space and time, looking in your world but still staying in the high energy of fifth dimension. My skill of thought makes the needed connections through this third dimension energy to the spirit within. When we learn to connect to light workers, we drop into the third dimension energy to make our connection, and then return to the fifth dimension energy. With this experience, we are supported with healing cleansing to help us clear any negative third dimension residue energy we have picked up.

Harry's parents Margaret and George lived in a terraced house in the East End of London, not far from the dockyards. George was a dock worker and at the time of Harry's birth, the country was in a recession and there was low employment everywhere. But George had been lucky with his dock work and the family had kept its head above the poverty line. I have to be honest – Harry was not really wanted when he was conceived, as they did not need another mouth to feed and put added pressure on their limited resources. But he won over their hearts as he was a contented baby, and they could not help but love him with his infectious cheeky smile.

When Harry was born his eldest brother Edward was twelve, then there was Peter aged ten, Catherine aged nine, Molly aged seven,

Mary aged four and Tommy aged two, and they were all cramped together in their terrace house. There was no bathroom, they washed at a bowl and had a hot bath once a week in a tin bath in the kitchen, and they had an outside toilet in the garden. The garden was not very big, but George enjoyed growing some vegetables to help with the food situation and ease their poverty. Their house was heated by coal fires and the coal was stored at the back of the house in a bunker and I remember seeing the coal carts on the cobbled street calling out as they were delivering. By the time Harry was one year old his brother Edward had got a part time job at the docks; the money wasn't much, but it all helped at home with the bills.

I admired his mother, she was a hard-working housewife who never wasted anything, and soups and stews were her forte. She also made most of their clothes and they were repaired to the point they could no longer hold another new repair patch or be darned. Most of the families around them were in the same situation so it was normal for the clothes to be a patchwork of repairs. But being a church-going lady, Margaret kept a Sunday best wardrobe for them all, always smartly pressed and clean, and this was passed down through the children as they grew. I remember watching Harry on his visits to the Christian church they attended, he found it very hard to stay still as he did not really understand why nearly every Sunday he was scrubbed from head to foot, squeezed into tight clothes and dragged to church. But what he did enjoy was when they got home, his mother always cooked the best meal of the week and afterwards, his father would have a drink and a smoke, then sleep. The children had to be quiet then so they were sent outside, but always back in their old clothes, and I knew this was the one time they all relaxed together in a busy working week. Their home was very basic, very busy, but clean; I also noticed that this was still a time when you left your doors open all day, and neighbours would pop for a gossip, while children played safely on the street outside.

Harry was a blond-haired, slim little boy full of mischief and laughter, with a kind heart. As Harry grew up I was around him more and more. He was poor but they were a happy family, and it was not really until he got to age eight that he started to get inner fears, as he heard his parents and other adults talking about a war. He felt the atmosphere change when this happened, and it affected his sensitive nature.

Being the youngest of seven, Harry never had anything new, apart from on his birthday, when his father would get him a cast iron car to add to his collection. Harry loved cars, he was very imaginative, and he wanted to build real cars one day. Harry's childhood routine revolved around school, playing on the streets and going to the docks with his friends to watch the ships come in. He did have some chores but somehow, being the youngest, the others often took them on, leaving him free to amuse himself more with his friends. The only thing that I felt really bothered Harry was that he needed glasses; his mother had noticed at a young age he struggled sometimes with his sight and she was proved right. The others teased him as no-one else in the family had glasses, but Harry knew he struggled without them, so learned to shrug it off. I observed that when a human is teased continuously the best thing for them is to ignore it, because the teasing stops when there's no reaction from the one being teased.

The first ten years of Harry's life had been those of a typical lad growing up in London, but his was slightly different with the background rumblings of a possible war. To Harry these were just words, and even though they worried him, he did not understand what they could mean to him and his family. When he was ten years old, his world changed around him. On September 1, 1939, Germany invaded Poland, which led Britain and France into war against Hitler's Nazi state on September 3rd 1939. Now, we had been watching this all unfold on Earth, preparing for this event and the return of many spirits within to their home existence. The guides like myself, with each human that would have contact with this war, were preparing to giving healing and guidance when needed and help the transition back home where necessary.

I remember this so well, the rumour of an announcement by the political leader of your time, Neville Chamberlain. Harry's family did not have a radio, so they went to a neighbour's, four doors up the street. The adults were in the front room of the house and sitting on the stairs, the children were filling in the gaps, and they all listened in complete silence at the announcement of the beginning of the

Second World War. As an observer of this I found it hard – the bewildered, worried faces of mothers, wives, fathers, husbands and young sweethearts not sure what all of this could mean to them. We did know what this could all mean for humanity and my heart ached for them all, for what humanity would have to go thorough yet again, having not learnt lessons from the First World War and many other Earth conflicts.

I now will mainly focus on how we saw this outbreak of war affect Harry and his family, so you can experience a more intimate viewpoint. His two older brothers, who at the outbreak of war were struggling to get regular employment, were called up into the armed forces. There was a day of excitement, upset and pride when they left to go to war. His mother and sisters were crying, Harry took his mother's hand to comfort her, and she held on to him tightly. His father could not fight due to an old leg injury, and it was decided his skills were needed for the docks and to help on the streets when there were bombing raids. His two older sisters got jobs in factories, replacing the male workers going off to war, and his mother stayed at home, giving her time over to knitting and making socks, gloves and hats which were sent to the front lines. Margaret was also very good with the rationing of food, but they had help; often George would get access to incoming foods, and small amounts that were filtered off, a bit like a black market between dockers, helped the local people – but this secret was kept behind closed doors.

After the announcement of war, Harry noticed how different the city felt. When he walked the streets, he didn't see many young men, and when he did, they were in uniform. The skies were full of barrage balloons and night spotlights streaming into the heavens. His house was blacked out at night so any German bombers would not target them with waste bombs. He liked to sneak out and watch the skies at night, wondering what the lights were looking for – then one night he found out, and it was a shock. A lot of the air raids had been away from the civilian population and more on the outskirts of London where the larger factories were. He heard talk of children being sent to the country because of fear of bombing raids, and wondered if that might happen to him; he was also aware of people who had the garden space, who were building air raid shelters. When the sirens went off, his family went to a local school called South Evansville; the basement there was deemed safe as the bombs usually fell a distance away and was only a distant worry to Harry and his family. When Harry's family was in the shelter, his father was often on the street supporting the Military Police (MP), and he joined them whenever he could, depending on the severity of the bombing.

One of the most traumatic days for his family was 7th September 1940, when the Germans decided to heavily bomb the East End of London docks. The Germans soon realised the docks were a key source of the country's supplies so made them a prime target. Up to this point, they had been strategy-bombing factories, RAF sites and power plants, but this soon changed. They decided it would now be OK to target civilian populations too. Some thought the civilian bombing happened by accident by stray bombs, but with the blitz style of bombing, it was soon apparent that this was not so. That evening when they went to the school basement, Harry knew the atmosphere was different, people were not playing games or chatting, there was fear in the air as they heard the bombs fall very near to the school, and it went on for a few hours. Harry did not get much sleep; his sisters were scared and he tried to comfort them, then the bombing stopped and there was silence and just the noise of sirens. Because the bombing had been bad, Harry's dad had been in the shelter that night as it was too dangerous on the streets. Harry's dad left the school at dawn to go and see what had happened. When he returned, he looked dirty and pale. Harry heard him tell his mother their home had been bombed and most of their street had gone, and it was too dangerous to try and go through the rubble yet for any possessions. His mum just sat and cried for what seemed to Harry an eternity. My heart went out to all those people, the heartbreak humanity was creating for each other, and I wrapped my energy round Harry to give the comfort I could.

As I looked at my fellow spirit friends supporting these people, we all saw any faith these people had in god disappear in those moments. They knew they had lost neighbours and friends as not all of them chose to go to the shelters because they believed god and their brick walls would protect them. In those few hours, I saw Harry lose his childhood innocence and become a confused, quiet little boy. He was scared but trying to be brave for his mother's sake, and wondering what the future held for them all.

They stayed in the upper levels of the school for the next day, as they now were homeless refugees and victims of the war. They were told they would be bussed out of London to somewhere safer, but Harry's dad would stay and help at the docks, and stay with a fellow dock worker until further notice. In this time frame, I was seeing families being ripped apart, never knowing when they would all be reunited.

As a guide observer I was noticing the difference in feelings at times of emotional trauma to the physical being Harry, compared to what I'd experienced as the spirit within. As a guide, I had stepped back a level, not being as exposed to the emotions; but from my experience with physical beings I had greater understanding of what I saw and how Harry felt. Harry was unaware of us, and we knew this would be the case; being so young, and with so much affecting his energy field he would not feel us, but our healing would protect the spirit within while they lived through all of this first hand.

On September the 9th the bombing continued and along with the rest of the refugees, Harry's family was told to stay in the basement, as it was felt the area where the school was located was safe. Harry's family hoped to be bussed out of London to safety in the next couple of days with the rest of the refugees at the school. Harry's family went to where their street used to be, this time his mother was silent; the shock had set in of losing everything apart from what they had taken that evening to the shelter. Harry was clutching the one toy car he had brought with him – the rest of his collection was now lost in the rubble, along with the rest of the family's belongings. There were still fires burning in the rubble and people digging for bodies, the air smelt of smoke and death, something no human or we will ever forget once experienced.

The next day, September 10th, they were told they were going to be taken out of London, to a safer place. Some were taken from the school in the day and Harry's family was expected to be on the next bus load to go, but the buses did not make it back before the bombing started up again. They were told it would be the next day before they could leave, and the safest place overnight was in the school basement. Harry was there with his mother, Molly, Mary and Tommy; Catherine was not there as she had had volunteered to help with the wounded at a medical station, and her father was working on the streets again.

Everyone was exhausted from two nights of bombing raids; this was another night of fear, as the bombing seemed heavier and louder this time, as they were closer. But this night the faith came back and we heard prayers for all those family friends to be kept safe in this awful time. Harry watched his mother pray, the inner strength of the human willing to fight again for all, and put their faith in an unseen force, even though they had lost their home. Then there was a loud explosion as a parachute bomb hit directly onto the school and the basement area caved in as the building above exploded and collapsed. Harry and his family would not have suffered as their lives were taken in this cruel act of humanity hurting one another. As Harry's spirit within and some of his family's joined us back home, they were all confused, but we led them back to the safety of their homes existence and for the healing they needed.

Conclusion - My first experience as a guide to a physical being was over. I had been led by my incarnation team to your time of war among humankind. As you know, my first true experience of this was as spirit within to Marceline in the Napoleon era. At this time of Earth's history, the strength of war was mainly based on manpower, hand-to-hand fighting skills and the strategy behind how the troops were deployed. The most skilled at this with enough manpower were the victors.

We have witnessed many wars among humanity over thousands of years, all developing and learning from your previous wars on how to improve the strategy and gain the power and land you crave.

When we reflected on the Second World War of Harry's time, we really noticed the difference in how humanity fought the war. As well as manpower, it was the weapons of supremacy in the air, sea and land and the strategic methods they used that won the battles. We saw in the other wars that it was mainly the troops who suffered the casualties, but in your last two world wars, especially the second, the civilians were greatly affected and displaced through fighting and use of these powerful new weapons. This is also seen in your modern wars, where whole populations are displaced.

What brought fear to the universe was when humanity discovered the nuclear bomb, a dark energy power that no being anywhere in the universe should have and use against others, but which humanity used twice in the Second World War. I cannot put into words how we all felt at what we witnessed on Earth. It was not just the bombs but also the persecution of a race that one leader chose to eradicate from his country of origin, with millions of lives displaced and murdered. We asked, what right has anybody got to persecute another, and say they are not worthy of living? We also see persecution amongst some races in humanity in your modern day, when you see others lower than yourselves and have no respect for them. You know we could have walked away at what we witnessed in Harry's time period, but we kept the faith with humanity that one day you would learn from these terrible mistakes. Our purpose is to help humanity and we realised this had got lost in our own process of trying to learn and ascend from our own Earth journey.

As we said earlier, the third dimension energy matrix stopped the human remembering the Earth mission, and the spirit within had to bring this forth to achieve their mission and ascension. But we were failing our missions due to our own pursuit of ascension, and forgetting the bigger picture, which was to bring peace, love and light to Earth. At this point we asked more highly ascended star beings in the fifth dimension, to join us on earth as spirit within and guides, because we needed a new perspective on humanity and Earth. We asked them to gather information from their missions that would help aid humanity to ascend. We are honoured to say they accepted and are now a key part of our work with Mother Earth.

We see so much good in each Earth person, but it seems there are times when the powerful leaders and strength of weapons draw you into the wars that most of you don't want, but you seem too weak to make the stand against this. If you made a stand, this could cause more fighting and frictions, because in the state of war the energies are so low it seems the only way forward for you to gain occasional peace. But that '**NO**' voice coming from inside you is your spirit within asking you to see the light and follow the peaceful path with your spoken voice and actions. Remember, there is always a peaceful solution to all things. Saying this, we did witness among humanity, in a time of crisis, a new bond forming because of the harm people were doing to each other, that humans would help each other in time of need no matter what their background or race. We found the crisis made all equal, which gave us and other high ascension beings hope to carry on with Earth, seeing good could prevail over the darkness.

After the war, when all the horrors were revealed and the full extent of the persecution of a race was understood, most of humanity was in disbelief and shock. We feel it takes a crisis for humans to see the bad in others and to bring out the good in you, but the human being does not learn from this. All of humanity needs to sing from the same hymnbook for peace, while the ones with '**Power over you**' – the powerful leaders – need to lead the way for peace. The humans under these leaders need to speak out about what they want for humanity, such as peace; you would be surprised by how many of you want peace and an environmentally safe world. But we know good, love and kindness will prevail on Earth as it does in the spirit realm, and a new world will begin. You need to break away from the third dimension energy plane that's holding you in the cycle pattern of ego, fear, anger and uncertainty. As I have said before, when this happens your ascension will have moved you into the fourth dimension energy plane, of deeper understanding for all.

The intergalactic council of beings decided that to help humanity move forward, we needed to change our strategy when amongst you. Up to this point we were trying to guide you and hoping you would understand the spiritual way, but this was no longer enough. So we started the process of bringing in humans with a higher-level frequency adjustment to their DNA, creating this when we join with them as the spirit within. We also affiliated with more ascended star beings. These newborns you have come to know as Indigo, Crystal, Rainbow or Star children. They are all programmed with a greater purpose on Earth, mainly to bring in the spiritual way of being and gather information to bring peace and unity to humanity. These people can be healers, mediums or humans living in a pure light and love existence by helping others; they are givers to humanity and the animal kingdom. I won't go into great detail about them, as there are lots of Earth books that explain their purpose here, but they are being sent to you to at a high rate of numbers now and we will continue to do this. We started this program after the Second World War; remember that throughout the western world in the sixties and seventies, all the peace campaigners popped up, hippy generations for equal unity living, and we saw how the world moved forward in a more neighbourly way. At this point, more high ascension beings also became more involved, monitoring the Earth and her progress, hence the high number of unexplained objects known as UFOs.

Over the last twenty years, the star children's frequency has been set higher to the fourth and fifth dimension energy levels and because of this they have been misunderstood, sometimes labeled as difficult children because their frequency has trouble adjusting to the third dimension energy field matrix. These children and adults can feel as if they don't belong on Earth or even fit in their own body. This is because the high love frequency energy vibration is trying to fit into the heavier third dimension energy vibration. But we have been working hard so that future star children will be able to adjust themselves to the energy around them and fit better within the human race. All these star children have an inner purpose that they know, and the spirit within and higher self helps them to recognise this and bring them forward on their spiritual path to help humanity. But these young beings still have free will, just a higher frequency of understanding with more support and guidance from us.

The good news is that more humans are remembering their mission and connecting to their Multidimensional spiritual energy. Now, if you are feeling this shift and being drawn to go to spiritual churches, fairs and workshops, then please listen to this inner guidance. Each step you take on this spiritual path is a step up the spiritual ladder of ascension, and this is part of your Earth mission. Trust what you learn, see, hear and feel as you develop – it is not your imagination. Allow yourself to acknowledge what you experience; this has not happened on Earth before, so you cannot refer to history books, you just have to TRUST us.

So yes, we are now influencing your Earth's path before you spiral into self-destruction, and it is all for the greater good. None of us wants Earth to perish; we have faith in the human sparks of love, kindness and unity that we have witnessed over millennia, for things to change.

Because of this newfound way of working with you all, and the experience I have gained as the spirit within, I felt my next physical being was to be a spirit within a star child. My family and overseers agreed with this and my next life plan was set in motion.

Chapter 8

Spirit within Sharon - *Earth*

My new ascension energies had balanced out nicely and all my spirit within and guide experiences had served me well and added new understanding to our knowledge pot. We were very excited at the new decision to bring more star children to Earth and start raising the planet's frequencies in phases, to help all of humanity ascend. I really wanted to be part of this new phase, a spirit within a star child who would have a life path to be a light worker. Actually, quite a few of us had this wish to help guide humanity towards the love and light that your world so needs. I was so happy when it was granted for me to take on this role – and it was to be with a human being called Sharon.

This young being Sharon has the star seed inside her, which affects her DNA so she can tune into other ascended beings. The ascended star people the Arcturians and Pleiadians chose to be part of her guide team from birth to gather information, learn from her life and eventually reveal themselves to her and others. They do this to spread love and light to all of humanity, but part of Sharon's Earth path was also to learn about rejection, family bonds, acceptance, reconciliation, forgiveness and the love you find when you have your soul mate. As you can imagine, this was all very exciting for us and we all looked forward to the physical journey with this human being.

May I also add here that star children come with more guides – on average there are seven with their Gate Keeper. The additional support is needed to deal with their higher-set frequency, sensitivity and all the guidance that they need to achieve their path here on Earth, which is so vital for humanity. It's also an opportunity for other ascended beings to observe the life and share their viewpoints at my healing debriefing, detailing what knowledge they found would help Earth.

This is the last chapter of my experiences as a spirit within and as I write this through Sharon, I am experiencing your modern world. It is very exciting for me to be part of your world as it is now and contribute to the transition that is taking place in humanity towards ascension. I will describe my time with Sharon so far, based on the spiritual journey she has had on earth, the experiences with her guides and me, with a hint of the human experiences that influenced her in to the character she is today.

Sharon came into your world in the summer of 1960 after a tiring labour. Her birth mother Jeanette had conceived out of wedlock. Sharon's father was a married man and sadly her mother had not realised this at first as she had been deceived, and when he knew she was pregnant he disappeared out of her life. Jeanette's own mother and father were shocked when she told them of her pregnancy. Now remember this was still the era when you did not have children out of wedlock in many countries in the eye of the church. It was thought to bring shame on the family mainly because of the Christian and catholic faiths. Jeanette's parents did not want the shame, but she did choose to keep the baby and had to leave her hometown and move to another city where she was unknown. For the rest of her pregnancy, she was taken into a home for unmarried mothers run by nuns. Apart from her parents, no-one knew where she was, not even Jeanette's younger brother Alan was unaware of her pregnancy; everyone thought she was working away from home.

Jeanette eventually took the decision to give Sharon up for adoption as she felt she could not provide the type of life for her she would wish for her. Gerald and Judith Hemming adopted her; her new mother was a housewife and her new father was in the RAF and had just been transferred to the area where she was born. Judith and Gerald had one natural son Clive, but they had lost some children through miscarriage and still-birth. Because of this, it was advised she had no more for her health's sake, so they had taken the decision to add to their family by adoption. However, two years later they were blessed with another natural son, David, and after that, due to the serious health complications of giving birth, Judith had to have a hysterectomy.

This was a new experience for me; the baby physical being Sharon did not have time to bond with her natural mother which is a wise decision because the memories of bonding stay deep-rooted with the human essence. I did feel the grief of the mother as she had to leave her daughter behind, but she knew she could not bring her up as she would have wanted and it was the best decision for the child. Jeanette went back to her old life, told everyone she had been away working and carried on with her existence, a little bit wiser and more weary of the human race.

And so my Earth life started as spirit within Sharon. Her father left the RAF when she was two, he was due to renew his commission but it was felt the RAF life had affected Judith's health too much, so he retrained as a teacher. This was a very hard decision as his heart was with his RAF life, he had been in the second world war as a squadron leader and his roots were deep set. As for Judith she carried on as the housewife but had a yearning to get a degree and be a social worker.

Sharon was a happy little girl, quite sensitive, with a knowing about people; she could sense their feelings and the atmosphere of a room even from a young age, because she was an empathic. As she grew and started to talk, she felt different from her brothers; she looked so different, with her shock of red hair against their dark brown, and she could not understand why, until her parents told her she was adopted. They explained what this meant, but at a young age she could not fully comprehend it all and thought this was why she felt different; but we knew she was also different because she was an empathic and a star child. She was also a real tomboy, always outside, and loved playing with her brothers' toys as well as her own. She could also be a bit mischievous, and that did get her into trouble a couple of times I have to admit.

To make sure you understand what an empathic is I will explain it here, because I also know some of you will see yourselves in this description. Being an empathic means you are affected by other people's energies and have an innate ability to intuitively feel and perceive others. Your life is unconsciously influenced by others' desires, wishes, thoughts and moods. Being an empathic is much more than being highly sensitive and it's not just limited to emotions. Empathics need to replenish their energies in nature, as they give so much else out to others, because they have huge hearts full of love.

Sharon was also a very creative child and loved drawing and doodling. She struggled at school from a young age and it was discovered at the age of nine she was dyslexic and number blind. You see, her high frequency setting had affected the wiring of her brain; she was bright and imaginative but struggled to understand her letters and numbers. I remember the day a vital person came in on her path, a new head teacher at her school. The head teacher was very experienced with dyslexic children, who were rarely understood back then, and she spotted Sharon, diagnosed her and helped her with one-to-one tuition. This memory stuck with Sharon even to this day, as her head teacher helped her understand the world around her a bit better so she could progress at school. The head teacher is an example of what we call Earth angels; they come into your life to help you at times of need, never to be seen again but always imprinted on your memory.

Sharon had an uninterrupted, happy upbringing in her early childhood, and it wasn't until she was aged about eleven that I saw the unsettling changes start in the family unit. Sharon went to her father's school and because of this, she was bullied. I saw how bullying can affect another human, it broke my heart to see it impact on her mental and physical state. She started to become withdrawn and pretended to be ill so she did not have to go to school. One day her parents sat her down and she told them about this one girl who was the main bully, with a group of friends who joined in as well. Sharon stopped it by standing up to the main girl; it took a lot of courage, her parents had gone to the school about it and of course her father was a teacher there, but even these factors did not stop the girl being a bully to Sharon and others, until Sharon faced her and stopped the bullying herself.

I'm not sure of the best way to handle bullies in your third dimension energy field. In this case it worked for Sharon, but for the purposes of ascension, sitting down and talking out the problems and looking at the backgrounds of the bullies is the real way forward. The bully usually has life issues that need to be dealt with and healed so they stop the behaviour, and I know in time humanity will stop behaving unkindly and aggressively towards each other. From this outcome, I saw Sharon gain more respect in her year group and became more popular; it was the only time she was ever unkind to another child. I do believe I saw the human primitive survival instant kick in with Sharon when she chose to take physical action to stop the bullying. It also meant that she could call on this life lesson when her own son became a victim of bullying. The advice she gave him was not to hit back, and she dealt with it through the school, and that eventually solved the problem. This was good for us to see, as it showed she had learnt that violence in life was not a productive way forward.

It was also around this time that her mother Judith took the opportunity to study for a degree and was not at home as much; at this time they employed an au pair for a while. I could feel Sharon felt unsettled for a time, but as with most things, she adapted. I did find it sad that also around this time her parents started to become heavy drinkers, which affected the mood and energy in the house. This was also the stage in Sharon's path when she started to become aware of spirit energy and her first experience was when she went on holiday with her family and stayed in an old cottage in Devon. When they pulled up outside the cottage, I was delighted to see Sharon knew it and had a different energy, but she was feeling frightened due to lack of understanding. She was picking up on a spirit energy that had not come back home yet, as her energy was held to this cottage where she had been murdered in the kitchen. (She has returned back to her home existence, now just to reassure you, but sometimes when life is suddenly taken, the spirit within is confused and thinks they are still alive in the third dimension energy matrix. They hold on to the physical human essence as they think they are this Earth being still. We do try to make them see otherwise but if they have a strong pull to the Earth energy through grief or love, it can be hard to achieve this and takes time. We are grateful to our medium friends that help us with this rescue work.)

As we entered the front room, I remember Sharon feeling uncomfortable, but the real feeling of fear was in the dining and kitchen area. She sensed that something powerful had happened there, and knew it was to a woman who had lived there. Sharon was supposed to sleep downstairs on her own, being the only girl, but she got so upset, she slept upstairs with her younger brother, where the energy was clear.

To us this was very interesting, as we now knew Sharon could sense spirit; she did not see or hear us yet, it was still all in the mind's eye. Children are born open to spirit, but for the lessons Sharon needed to learn in life, which would help with her spiritual ascension in later life, we let her develop as most other children do on Earth, where this spirit connection is suppressed. There are rare cases where some of your world mediums have had full-on spirit senses and experiences all the way through their lives; this just means their learning path was different.

As I observed Sharon in her childhood, it was interesting to see how she reacted to the Christian faith. She was a Brownie then a Girl Guide, and did not enjoy the Sunday services she found herself attending. She felt there was a falsehood to religion that was based on fear – if you are not good you go to hell – she felt these teachings were false and should all be based on love. She also believed in aliens and UFOs and as she grew into her teen years, she became quite interested in this subject; with the ascended star people influence around her we expected this to happen. She also felt Jesus Christ was actually a highly ascended alien who visited earth!! There was no one around her telling her these beliefs, it was coming from her star seed DNA and from me, her spirit within.

The next unusual spiritual experience was when she was fourteen. Her older brother, whom she was very close to, was now eighteen and looking at going to university in Southampton. Her mother took him down to visit and Sharon went too. While he was looking around the university they went shopping, and as she was walking along the high street, she froze; we had taken her back a hundred and fifty years or more on the timeline. She saw similar but older buildings, carts and carriages, a muddy road with straw on it, and a well-to-do lady with a slave child in tow. She was bought out of this trance state by her mother calling her name, and as we intended, the memory of that day never left Sharon, and sparked an interest in time travel and past lives. She did often wonder if she had imagined it, but she knew deep down it was a glimpse of Southampton in the past.

During these early years of her teens, her mother became more controlling and dictatorial. Some of this was due to frustration over her own life and alcohol. Her parents had drifted apart as people without much in common and there were more arguments within the home. Sharon really did not cope with these well, locking herself away in her room or going for a walk. Sometimes when it was too much she would shout at them to stop, and she found this hard to bear when her older brother went to university, as he was her rock at home.

This was such a mixed up emotional time for Sharon, being led by others and made to feel it was a life she did not feel at home in. She was persuaded by her parents to join the young conservatives for a social life, and at the same time she was told that she could only mix with white people. She felt very out of place as this was not the way she felt or thought; these were the ideas of her controlling parents – both of them were very strict, but her mother more so. Her parents had had similar experiences as young people, and believed this was the correct way to bring her up. This did affect the emotional side of Sharon's being, which manifested later in her life when she had children. What her parents did not know is that she had some Indian friends at school she never told them about. It was sad for me to see Sharon could not be her true self, yet these were lessons she had to learn from as we observed.

When Sharon was seventeen she changed her mind about religion and discovered Jesus again, and she wore hippie skirts and played guitar and loved singing religious songs. She and her friends frequented places where groups spoke in tongues and worshipped Jesus and God. To her, it was a release from home life with a happy higher energy, which got her away from her parents' negative energies. Around this time, she also had a very good friend who asked her to join in a Ouija board at her house with her friends. Her friend lived in an old house that had residue spirit energy, which is why Sharon sometimes felt uneasy in it, as she could sense it. We guided her not to be involved in this as was going to be run by inexperienced girls who did not know what they were doing and could attract unwanted energies to them. Sharon chose not to join her friends and it was good for us to see Sharon was getting our telepathic thoughts and acting upon them.

Her journey with worshipping the figurehead Jesus carried on for a year or so until one day, she and her best friend decided to try out a new church they had heard about. They turned up for the service, but were taken off to a side room, and asked if they were willing to get on their knees to confess their sins before they could join the church. Well, we set off alarm bells for her, telling her to get out of there, and they both did. Sharon then realised she was experiencing the fear-based religions again – confess your sins or go to hell. She had no sins to confess, and the people of the church were using their human power and dominance in the name of religion.

It was also around this time that Sharon had her first UFO encounter. One day in her hometown she was walking towards the town centre when she looked up and saw a pulsating light object moving slowly on a distant tree line. She thought it was a small plane, then it suddenly darted back and forth a few times, then darted quickly to the right, hung in the sky for several minutes without moving, then shot off at high speed into space and disappeared. It was good to observe, as Sharon thought it was another of her **'did I imagine it'** moments - but she did not. That week in the local paper, UFO sightings were reported which confirmed to Sharon she had not imagined this amazing event in her life. She had always known aliens were out there and could never explain why; so we were pleased to show her a star ship from one of our highly ascended being friends helping us with Earth. They are around all the time but they keep themselves veiled from you in the higher dimension frequency, but don't be alarmed – they are here to observe and guide humanity and as guides to chosen earthlings.

One of the turning points in Sharon's life was at the age of nineteen when she went to Art College in her hometown. Through this she discovered just how controlled and sheltered her upbringing had been, because all of a sudden she was mixing with all nationalities and cultures and she loved the diversity of it. She found she could have her own opinions and not be afraid to voice them. I observed this change in Sharon with interest as she became more confident and more outspoken at home – which did not go down well with her controlling parents.

In this life-changing year she had her third spirit encounter. She got a job in a local pub and worked in the public bar. This job suited Sharon, as she liked meeting and talking to people. Where she stood waiting to serve people was a narrow space, so that for anyone to get by her, she would have to move out of the way. She had been working there for a couple of weeks when one night she felt two hands on her hips and she was gently pushed out of the way. I still remember her facial expression when she realised no-one was there – she was actually quite shocked. She made some inquiries and the landlord told her they had seen some activity in the bar area – a shadow had been seen walking there and in the kitchen, and it had started since they had done some building work upstairs in the pub. Again, this was another experience we were pleased Sharon had felt, because to be physically moved by spirit takes a lot of energy from us. You might wonder why we kept giving her spiritual experiences like this at spaced-out intervals but you will understand later on, my friends.

With her parents still trying to control her life, things came to a head when Sharon met her soul mate, Chris, at college. Her parents wanted her to marry, let's say, a doctor or lawyer; they had not envisioned a nineteen-year-old boyfriend with long hair, tie-died clothes washed in the student clothes boiler with a motorbike. I am laughing while I think about this time and remember the day well, when they invited him round for a formal dinner; their facial expressions and thoughts were not happy ones. Sharon and Chris were in love; in Sharon's eyes, he was the nicest chap you could meet and from what I observed, he was. Sadly, Sharon's parents did not take to him and one day they gave her an ultimatum – to choose them or Chris. I will never forget the day Sharon left her home after a huge row; she ran all the way to Chris's halls of residence and never looked back. She then became estranged from her family; only her older brother kept in touch as they were close, and her life carried on without much contact with the rest of them.

On a serious note, I know I said I was laughing but that is because Sharon's parents' spirits within higher self's and myself have reflected on some of those moments and have to find humour sometimes to raise our energies, as it's so sad how through the actions of others, families can become estranged. The one thing we all need is love and support. Sharon found this from her soul partner and his family, but should have had it from both families and partner. This is a lesson for all of you in learning acceptance of others and letting people live their own lives.

Sharon married her long-haired biker and they bought their first home together after a couple of years. This is where she experienced her fourth spirit encounter. They had an old terraced cottage that they nicknamed 'The Refresher Row', as all the houses were painted in the colours of the sweets; and theirs was pink. I also had realised this was how they would live their lives together in the energy of fun. For this experience we chose to bring back to the house the energy of a gentleman who used to live there and waited for when they put stairs into the basement and started renovating it. The reason for this is it changed the energy flow of the house and we could work with it better.

Sharon at first thought she was having dreams, but they were waking moments of seeing the form of our spirit friend standing at the top of the landing looking into their room. She saw that he was dressed in middle-class Victorian clothes, with dark, collar-length hair and a hat. A couple of times, she felt as if she was being held down in the bed or someone was leaning over her; this was his spirit energy drawing close to her, but as it frightened her we stopped that. There were also times when her two cats would follow him with their eyes, then dart out of the cat flap at high speed, this was to help her realise she was not the only one seeing him. Sharon was learning to play the piano at this time; she was not a natural musician I must add, but we liked to stand behind her and observe her as she tried, and she felt our presence. We chose for Chris to never feel or see anything, to help build Sharon's trust in her own intuition. Sharon only told one other person apart from Chris, which was a friend at work, as it played on her mind. Then one day an old friend came to stay; she had not told her of her gentleman spirit visitor. A few months later, they went to stay at her house and they were talking about ghosts and so on, and her friend said, *"You know you have one? I saw him at the top of the stairs."* After that, Sharon accepted him as real and then became less aware of him, but felt he just popped in now again to see how they were doing and she knew he meant them no harm.

They had five happy years in this house, with their two cats Sam and Ben. I do remember a very emotional period during this time when Sharon got the urge to trace her birth family. She had gone to her birth town with her adoptive mother in 1978, and got all the papers on her birth and adoption. She discovered the birth name of her mother, but no father's name was on the original birth certificate. Her birth mother had a very rare surname, so it did not take her long to find who she thought were some family members. One day, they took the courage to ring a number she found, and she asked Chris to do this, as she was nervous. When he rang he spoke to a lady, and told her they were looking for Jeanette and had a message for her. The lady said she knew Jeanette and would tell her he had rung, and took down Chris's phone number. But there was never a call back. Little did they know at this time that he had spoken to Sharon's natural grandmother, but it was to be years later when Sharon realised this.

By this time we were really pleased with Sharon's progress and her recognition of this spirit. We felt we would gradually build her awareness and we could then see the best way we could develop her as a light worker, as you are all unique, and so our journey continued. We wanted her to experience the emotional lessons of her Earth mission before we launched fully into the light worker section of her life. This is because emotions of sadness, fear and anger affect your ability to connect to the fifth dimension energies.

Sharon was very happy with Chris, but I could see her inner pain as she was still estranged from her adoptive parents. On the rare occasions they spoke, her adopted mother was either not pleasant or still trying to control the situation. Sharon found this hard to cope with and her natural human protection mechanism meant she removed herself from their lives for a while so they did not hurt her anymore. Sharon and Chris's journey through life took them to live in the city of Edinburgh with their jobs. They rented a top floor flat in a lovely Georgian block and this was where Sharon experienced her fifth spirit encounter. She would often hear children laughing and playing when she was climbing the stairs, or sometimes when she opened her flat door. There were no children in the block of flats, and Sharon made enquiries a couple of times, but what she was hearing was the energy residue of a time when children played and laughed in the old nursery rooms. We found her energies were getting more attuned and we were very pleased she picked up on this and could hear them. Sharon was not scared when this happened, it just intrigued her, which is what we hoped for.

They loved the city of Edinburgh and they were blessed with the birth of their first son Michael while living there. After five years, their life took them back to their hometown in the Midlands and during this time, they had another wonderful son Charlie. Their move was part of their life's path and a time in their lives where Chris's family would need them nearby for support. His brother and sister both emigrated to America and Canada, and then his father died, leaving his mother to cope alone. During this time, Sharon also suffered from depression after her second child, which her doctor said was caused by grieving for all the family changes and the loss of her father in-law. I found this all hard to bear for her, and we kept close, giving the healing that was needed from spirit to help her. Then after eighteen months, in the year 1998, Chris had an amazing job offer in the Gloucestershire area and they could not afford to turn it down. After the move it all proved too much for Sharon, and her depression really took hold. She had no one to talk to, and I witnessed a very sad, depressed being with plummeting energies.

Then one day it all came to a head and we witnessed Sharon sitting on the stairs in their rented house, with her two sons sitting below her and she could see no way out of the darkness that was enveloping her, except by ending her own life. At this moment I summoned her angels, as this was not her path; the darkness of the depressed mind can cause this and we cannot always stop it, so we willed her to seek help. She rang Chris, but he was in a meeting, so we then led her to ring a help line, and they advised her to go to the doctor straight away. Sharon then rang the doctors' surgery, crying and explaining she needed help, and was seen by a wonderful understanding doctor that same day. She was quickly referred to a psychologist and was diagnosed with severe postnatal depression. The human medical support she got was wonderful to see, and with the mixture of modern day drugs and counselling she turned a corner. In Sharon's case it was a combination of her childhood and adult controlling mental abuse, mainly from her mother that sat deep inside, with the added factor of hormonal chemicals and the change in her husband's stable family unit that caused her depression. It took her five years to recover from this fully, and rediscover her old human self.

We did everything to help with this from our high dimensions. I had never witnessed this kind of depression and darkness in the human mind before and received a lot of support from her guides and angels. This did delay her spiritual journey, as we had to make sure her energies were back up at full strength to carry on. It was in her path to heal from her childhood mental abuse, but the human body and mind frame varies with you all and in Sharon's case we had not foreseen the deep dark depression into which she would withdraw.

Sharon had further spiritual experiences that manifested as general feelings of uneasiness; she was sensing spirit, but not sure what it was. The sixth spirit experience that really struck her was after her sister-in-law Anna died from lung cancer, which was caused by heavy smoking. When Anna's higher self use to visit Sharon, she would get up in the morning and start her day by having two cigarettes and a coffee to get going. After her passing, for a few years on and off, Sharon used to get a smell of cigarettes, always in her hallway and lounge entrance. Sharon used to make me laugh, as she used to open the front door or back door to see if the smell was elsewhere, and check her sons were not smoking in the house. But it never was, as it was Anna's spirit visiting her, as a test for Sharon's reaction to a smell from spirit. She did eventually realise what was happening, as Anna's name popped into her head every time she smelled the smoke, and it was wonderful for us to see her acceptance of this.

By this time in Sharon's life, her awareness and energy levels had changed for the better, and she was very open to other people's energies, whether alive or as spirits. One example of this was when her father was dying. Sharon and her two brothers rushed to their father's hospital bedside because he had had a severe stroke and was given a few hours to live. Sharon knew his spirit was gone from the body, but his spirit within was stood nearby watching and waiting, while some small essence kept him bound to his physical body on the Earth plane. Thirty-six hours later, he was still breathing shallowly, after stopping and restarting a few times. Sharon asked the doctor why he had not passed yet; he said it could be that the part of the brain for breathing was still intact after the stroke. It suddenly came to Sharon when she was on her own with her father, that he did not want her to see him die, and she was right. Her father was an old-fashioned gentleman who felt she should not witness his death, while his sons could, as men of the family. Sharon said her goodbyes and told him to let go of the Earth plane, which he did a couple of hours later when her brothers were with him.

Up to this point in her lifetime, we had shown Sharon various ways in which spirit can show itself – she smelled a spirit, saw spirit, felt one's energy push her, and she was learning to sense them around her as her energies changed. Sharon's life continued to be good with just the occasional experience of sensing presences from the spirit realm. Her interest in angels, spirit, aliens and UFOs grew, and she fuelled this interest by reading books, and watching sci-fi films and documentaries on these subjects.

We could see by your year 2004 that the spiritual path for Sharon was now taking momentum so we stepped up our pace and started placing signs and opportunities on her path for her to see. Of course, at this point she had no idea that her graphic job and business would be a basis for the next adventure on her spiritual journey. It took a few Earth years but we really got started around March 2007, when Sharon's and Chris's advertising business moved out of the home to a local office space on a nearby farm. We placed her next to a holistic healer called Mary, and Sharon was delighted to discover this. Over a few weeks she got to know Mary, who was a crazy, wonderful lady. She was one of the few people Sharon had ever told about her spiritual experiences, dreams and what she felt about the worlds beyond Earth, and Mary did not think she was crazy.

I've just realised that I haven't mentioned dreams. Whenever one of Sharon's relatives or friends died we would send them to her in a dream to say they were OK, and it was interesting to observe that she did interact with them. She would also see them in the distance, but not be able to get through the veil to speak to them. You see, we use your dreams a lot to bring communication and guidance. The last time we did this to help Sharon make a connection to spirit was about nine years ago when her neighbour died; after a couple of weeks Sharon dreamed she was looking at him sitting outside in a hot climate at a table, he looked tanned and healthy. She asked him why he was there but he did not speak. She asked again and he laid down a card. When Sharon read it, it said, 'tell my wife I love her'. After wards Sharon could not get this out of her mind, and eventually she asked his wife round for a drink. After a couple of glasses of wine she told her about the message and his wife was very pleased to hear it. Sharon had hesitated, as she did not know how his wife would perceive this. If you receive a message in a dream, please pass it on, as we would not let you give anything out that is not needed. Even if the recipient seems unsure, you have done the right thing – be guided by the intuition that comes from your spirit within. Leaping forward in time, we are now using her dreams to introduce her star friends to her, an exciting time for us, I can tell you.

As a seed of interest and to help Sharon take notice of the beings in the higher dimensions, we gave her a repetitive dream through her life, which she felt she had lived but was not of the modern age she was in. The dream was a glimpse of my time as spirit within Marceline. In the dream, Sharon would be visiting a black gravestone and vault, and also had glimpses of a large drawing room, a hall with lots of paintings and a bedroom she did not want to enter. Sharon and Mary got to know each other over cups of tea and one day she told her about the dream she had had for years, and that she felt she had lived it, but not in this lifetime. Mary was trained in past life regression and asked Sharon if she would have this experience with her, and Sharon nervously agreed. *This was the point we had been waiting for, as this past life regression sparked her interest in mediumship and the high ascension energy beings.* Sharon has had more past life regressions since this first one, all showing her a glimpse of my spirit within existences. The one that really stood out to her was when she realised she had had a past life not on Earth, but on another world. All of this was our way of fuelling her imagination, energies and mind to help her on her spiritual journey, in the hope she took the right path.

From her meetings with Mary, Sharon was guided to do her Reiki One Course with her. We bought Reiki to Mother Earth so we can attune light workers to the higher energies and help you heal any individual anger and fears to aid raising your energies so you can work with us. This was such a powerful day for Sharon as she was touched by high ascension energy, and this led to her starting to forgive her adoptive mother for her actions against her, and started to heal. We let her see us in the Reiki room as our source of light pure love beings and auras round people, and she knew that what she was seeing were her guides and angels. We have not shown ourselves in this way again as she learnt to recognise our energies and TRUSTS we are there. This experience led Sharon to join Mary's Reiki and meditation circles, which really gave us a chance to work with her and see how she could pick up on our energies and messages to her.

Something I should share with you is that you start to change on your journey and connect with us; this is because your energy is lifted to a more positive vibration, you see your world with more clarity, and you seem different to those that know you well. You start to realise you are actually a fifth dimension being living in a restricted third dimension energy plane. All of this change will affect your energies and the people not ascending as you are will see you differently and not understand the change. This can affect your relationships with family and friends.

You become excited, lifted and more positive, good things start to happen to you, and not everyone will be pleased about this; some won't agree with your newfound life style and some will be jealous of your happiness. I saw this happen to Sharon when she lost a friend of eighteen years on her early journey, and this did affect her greatly. However, at the same time it prepared her for further occasions, as this was to happen again, a few times in the future. Sharon realised that anything that did not serve her, for example jealousy or manipulative people, fell away from her life, helping to bring the positive, loving people in that were needed on her true path.

While this entire spiritual journey was happening, Sharon, after her father died, decided to search for her real parents. She found out her mother had remarried and had two further children, Grant and Simon, also a uncle and cousins. This was such an emotional time to witness and we had to give Sharon extra support and healing while on this life discovery. Her mother did not wish to meet her, but she met her half-brothers a couple of times and they have stayed connected through your technology. Her uncle excepted her as part of his life and Sharon became close to his eldest daughter. Her birth Nan died not long after this; they never met, but her higher self is now part of Sharon's journey while in spirit. She has come through a few times now to give some advice and guidance, the key message being that Sharon would never meet her birth mother while she was on the Earth plane – a message that Sharon, with her faith and understanding of the spiritual journey, has accepted and understood. I think what I learnt most from this experience was that the human being needs to feel they belong, and know where they are from. Your DNA does not just bring through your looks, but also your personality, and even habits that can be inbred deep within the roots of the DNA. So when adoptive people meet up with family it can be quite amazing how similar they can be, even in the gestures they make. We knew that everything Sharon experienced in this search would be used later in her life to help others in readings, drawing on her understanding of the emotions that can be experienced in these situations. Remember that there is a reason for every experience you have, a learning curve to help you through your life.

When Sharon did her Reiki level two, I saw her experience learning more about what Reiki can do to help others. At the same time, she was healing and clearing the emotional pain caused by her adoptive mother and was now ready to channel for spirit our healing divine energy. Sharon had held so much guilt and hurt about her mother that unless she healed, it would keep her energies low and affect how we could work with her. At the time of her adoptive mother's death Sharon had not seen her for a long while; her mother had lung cancer that they believed had spread up from her ovaries, and she did not have long to live. Her older brother asked her to go to the hospital and Sharon drove to see her, juggling a lot of unsaid emotions and words on the way. When she got to her bedside, she saw a frail, sick woman, a shadow of the former woman she had feared yet loved. She held her hand and their eyes met; words were not needed, and forgiveness was there. She left the hospital and never saw her mother alive again; she died a few days later. Sharon had always wondered if her mother had understood that all was at last OK between them. We gave her confirmation, in 2016, through a platform medium's message that her mother had understood when Sharon was at her deathbed. The reason we waited was that Sharon had to have forgiven her mother completely, herself, which was the final closure. The human part of Sharon did not realise how much she needed this message, and even though emotional she was elated to have received it.

Sharon carried on in the development circles, becoming more interested in mediumship, and then one day at Mary's centre, she attended a mediumship workshop. The morning was on a psychic level, but in the afternoon they took it in turns to connect to spirit clairvoyantly with the help of the medium, and bring in a loved one. Her husband was there that day to support her, as Sharon was quite nervous about this new adventure, and he was surprised when she connected with his dead cousin and her adoptive mother. It was a WOW moment for us – her light was shining brighter as a new beacon for spirit.

We realised afterwards that the only downside had been the teaching medium neglecting to instruct the class about shutting down their energies and protection. In some ways, this helped us see what Sharon would hear, feel and see, but also it worked against us, as she was a bit fearful of the next experiences she encountered. She started to hear voices in the house at night, see shadow figures, and in bed at night, she felt as if spirit was queuing up in the bedroom to see her. Her eldest son was seeing a young girl and a shadow figure of someone in his bedroom. Sharon's energies started to drop and she got very tired, so we thought it best she got some guidance, and led her back to her Reiki Master Mary. Mary told her that she needed to shut down to them and helped her to understand the importance of self-protection and taking control, so that is what they did. We know this stopped her connection with spirit, but it was more important to protect the chosen Earth being so we can complete our mission with her.

Sharon did not go on the Reiki journey ever thinking she would practice and earn money from it. She was just very intrigued by it all and was one of those Reiki babies who felt she could not charge for this spirit gift we gave to others. One of the things I realised was that her Reiki journey had made her re-evaluate her life, and work-life balance. At this time she worked with her husband in his advertising business, but she wanted to be more creative and work from home. So she started to create a business making wedding guest books in her spare time. We realised that Sharon was so creative that she needed to channel this, and this was when she was happiest and her energy high, so we set a plan for her to be able to achieve this. During this period, she saw a medium for a reading at Mary's holistic centre. She was amazed at this reading, with her relatives and friends popping in to say hello. We gave the medium two messages for her. First, she was to continue with her creative path and second, spirit would be waiting for her to come back to mediumship when she felt ready. Well, Sharon's ego laughed at the latter, but we knew this was her path.

Mary's centre had to close for various reasons, which freed up Sharon's time to concentrate on the creative route of the wedding books business. It took off, and she realised she had created a business that became nearly a full time job. She was so busy with life that she did not look elsewhere to continue her spiritual path, but carried on reading about angels, UFOs and medium life stories, and watched all of those types of programmes on TV when she had the chance.

During the time Sharon set up her new business, Chris's advertising business moved back home because it had felt the impact of a worldwide recession. She still had some involvement, handling admin and some graphic work. After a couple of years, we decided it was time to lead Sharon back to us so we started to leave signs for her to pick up on.

Around the year 2014, her husband's health took a turn for the worse; he had a bleed in his eye through high blood pressure and diabetes spiking. This affected his work and their income; he felt depressed, and it was a tough period for both of them to endure. During this time Sharon felt unwell too; she lived with fibromyalgia, so was used to experiencing dips in health, but this was different, so eventually she took myself off to see the doctor. After some tests and seeing a consultant, she discovered that she had extremely high cholesterol and non-alcoholic liver disease. Sharon was very overweight and unfit as well. Through the doctor's guarded words she realised she had to get fit or her future health would decline, so we guided her to join the village gym to lose weight, and little did she know that this was the next part of her spiritual journey.

When Sharon joined the gym, she met ladies she had not seen since her two sons were at primary school. There was one in particular with whom she became friendly; every time she saw her she kept getting the words Reiki, Reiki, Reiki running through her head. Yes, it was us at work again. She was reluctant to offer Reiki as she only had a small room and a chair to do it in, but the feeling would not go away and one day she asked her friend Susan if she would like some Reiki to help de-stress her, free of charge of course. Her friend jumped at the chance; through this others started to hear about the healing and its benefits, and they asked for Reiki too. She still could not get her head around charging for Reiki but started to realise she would like to provide a holistic service. This was a breakthrough for us and led the way for us to spark the mediumship interest in her too.

Our next plan along her life path was to guide her to see a very experienced local medium. Without knowing this, Sharon was drawn one day to see a local medium on platform at a local venue. Sharon loved her when she saw her on platform and emailed her afterwards to see if she taught or mentored people for mediumship - she knew from her first experience that she could not go back to mediumship without guidance and support. The medium kindly put her in touch with a wonderful lady from a Spiritualist Centre in the area, where Sharon went one night to an open mediumship development circle – and the next stage of her spiritual journey could really begin.

Sharon found it quite funny that we had guided her to a new spiritual centre that was based in a horse-stable business in a converted barn. Sharon is allergic to horses, which she discovered when she was learning to ride at the age of seventeen! There were two ways this could have gone for us: Sharon's ego could have stepped in and said, 'stay away from the horses', or, as we hoped, she could see this as a sign she was in the right place. Fortunately, it was the latter – Sharon felt very at home at this centre and was made very welcome. She sat in the open medium development circle, attending occasional healing circles and workshops. Sharon's human mind was dreaming of being a platform medium; we knew this was on her future path, but were other plans for her to fulfil before this.

In March 2015, we guided her to attend a trance workshop at the centre; this was an amazing day for Sharon and she became fascinated by trance. During the day, she practised meditation, where we introduced her to her main Gate Keeper guide, a monk called Harold. He showed himself to her with a writing feather in his hand, sitting at a desk surrounded by scrolls, and through his telepathic thought he was encouraging her to write. I should add that Sharon was already doing inspirational writing as part of her development, but as she was dyslexic, she let her mind think that she would struggle with this and any form of writing. To her surprise, after this workshop, her writing started to really develop and flow freely with deep wisdom. Harold was already familiar to Sharon because in her Reiki days she had been aware of a guide who was a monk. She now knew that after being a bit frightened of the unknown, there was nothing to be scared of, as Harold had made her feel he was wise and would be very patient with the writing, and always look after her.

By the end of 2014, Sharon knew she wanted to run a holistic business, and in January 2015, with our encouragement, she set up Bengalrose Healing. I knew she was not confident, not to mention scared and unsure, but knew she was being guided to do this; and as with all jobs, you only gain experience from working and learning. Sharon offered free Reiki and readings for two months, so she could gain some work experience and build a reputation. What she learnt in those two months was that everything she did was with the intent of healing and creating wellbeing for her clients. She realised her readings would bring about healing for them, guidance and closure, and the Reiki also helped with healing and de-stressing her clients. We were so pleased to see that she now knew this was her path and was what she wanted to do in her life.

Around this time, Sharon's husband's health was still poor, and he was very unhappy. Although this was affecting her energies, she carried on with her holistic passion, but found it difficult as her ego was making her feel guilty about doing something she loved while he was a bit lost in his life. Because of this, we guided Sharon to attend a workshop called 'The Miracles of Life.' This workshop focused on shifting the blockage that is holding someone back, and changing the way they think to create those desired miracles in life. Part of the day was spent writing a list of things they needed to release that were holding them back, and attaching the names of those involved. These lists were then burnt under the power of prayer to release any attached emotion, fear, anger and hurt over to the universe and us. After Sharon did hers, I witnessed her experience an overwhelming rush of emotion as she realised that the one thing that was holding her back had not been put on the list. She realised that she was considering putting her holistic and mediumship journey on hold so she could help her husband find his path and be happier, but she did not want to stop her own spiritual journey.

She spoke to a friend who pointed out to her that sometimes, you have to naturally shed those that hold you back, including loved ones, when you are on a spiritual journey. Well, that made Sharon think! She wanted her husband to be happy and she wanted to be happy too. Sharon was of the character that would reflect on things and this helped us to guide her. This was key, because her spiritual journey was also going to trigger journeys for other people close to her on her path in the future. Sharon took note of what she had learned in this workshop, firstly, to imagine and feel she was living in the future she wanted, which included her husband being well and in a job, and feeling valued again. After a couple of weeks, we were pleased when she decided to face this issue head-on with Chris, and took him out for a pub meal. She told him about what had happened at the workshop, and he needed to start thinking positively to move on with his life. He admitted he was very down and he saw her soaring ahead, and he felt he was being left behind. We influenced Sharon to ask him, *"What is the one thing you really want to do?"* and he said, *"Painting, and to be an artist."* She then asked him what was stopping him. He said, *"I am afraid of failure."* Chris realised at this point he was blocking his own path, and preventing himself from moving forward. We were pleased Chris saw this, as this was a shift on his own spiritual path as well as Sharon's.

We then guided Sharon to go on a mediumship retreat, as she needed some space away from her day-to-day life to refocus and develop her link with spirit. It was lovely for us to see her so happy. She did miss her home as she is what you call a home bird, but the experience she gained outweighed this for her. On the Saturday afternoon during a tea break, she checked her phone and there was a message from Chris. She clicked on it and her eyes popped – there was a painting of her dog Boyd. YES! Chris had done a painting! This was such a special moment for us to witness, as he had gone through his own barrier of fear. Sharon rang him and when she spoke to him, she could hear a difference in his voice and he sounded more uplifted. She felt such relief for him and for herself too, as she knew this was a sign she could carry on with her light worker's journey, not worrying about him, because he was getting himself back on his life's path. From Chris making these positive changes and way of thinking, he got a contract of work, which brought them financial security, and he carried on with his painting. His leap forward cleared the way for Sharon to build her holistic business, as they were now more financially secure.

When you take the spiritual path it will affect the world around you, especially in friendships and relationships. Don't fear this, as you will shed the negativity and draw the positive and better people nearer to you. Also note, people do not go out of your life for good; they stay there as part of your everyday existence, but they are more in the background as you learn to protect yourself from the negative energy they bring in. As with the story of Chris, you can help others excel on their life's path without holding yourself back.

We carried on working behind the scenes with Sharon and helping her with her spiritual development. I feel this next story in her lifeline shows you well how we do this.

Sharon went on a second weekend retreat which involved working with spirit in workshops, and as large groups over two days, and it was an awesome experience for her and us. On the Sunday morning, we woke her early at 5.30 am, and she heard a single birdsong outside her window; she tried to go back to sleep but we made her feel hot and restless and she decided she needed some fresh air. She went outside and watched the sun start to creep over the horizon, and a gentle warm glow appeared in the morning sky. She sat there in the morning chill and watched the sun come up, the birdsong got louder and louder, and the peace of the world was broken as she watched a few clouds gently floating by. As Sharon sat there she reflected on her spiritual journey, her self-doubt, her husband's health, and being scared she would lose him in death.

After this time of reflection in the beauty of the morning sunrise, we inspired Sharon to write some words from us.

The magic of the sunrise

As the sun rises in the stillness of the morn
Mother Earth takes a breath of the divine
The light shining across the lands
Awaking all life old and to be born.

The light beams awaken the silence
The chorus of life sings out again to you
The stillness now has movement and a voice
Your heart is awakened to Mother Earth's tune.

As the sun rises into the protection of the Earth
Your spirit stretches out to feel its warmth
Your body absorbs its life-giving energy
You find your path and life's worth.

As the sun sinks slowly below the horizon

The silence falls again on your spirit within
Know, my friends, you can hear our voice
In the silence there is love held frozen.

Sit in the silence and listen
Hear the night sound of the universe
Connect to the divine light beams
You will shine, sparkle and glisten.

Sharon reflected on these words; she felt they were very meaningful to her journey and thanked us for the inspiration. Well, we were now on a roll and later that morning she attended a workshop after an amazing trance session that left her very elevated. The workshop was based around music; prior to coming, the teacher had drawn up a list of forty-four songs and the names of the attendees, and had asked her guides to pick a song for each of the attendees. They then had to listen to the song and words, reflect on its personal significance at that moment in time, and then reveal this to the group. When it came to Sharon's turn she listened to the words; we witnessed a massive rise of emotion inside her, and she started crying. The song was called *'All things must pass'* and here are some of the words from the song so you can get a feel for why it affected her so much. The song mentioned *sunrise, cloudbursts, love, don't give up, everything passes, moving on* and *facing another day*. You can see from some of the words how it linked with Sharon's dawn experience. She had never heard the song before that day. It had struck a chord with her and with me as her spirit within and it helped us release the fear she was holding inside, and Sharon felt it and knew that everything would be OK. We needed to discharge these feelings in order to shift her energies, which would make her stronger, and able to forge better links with us.

We knew Sharon had understood what had happened to her, as the next day when she was back at home, she got up early again and walked one of her dogs as the sun came up. She played the song and felt inspired and at peace with the world around her. This was lovely, as we knew she had felt our love and healing and the caring way we love to work with you all, to bring what's needed to move forward with your spiritual journeys.

Since we've been working with Sharon and her first trance experience when Harold came in, we have managed to channel a set of daily guidance cards, and a spiritual book, 'Utopia', and at this stage of her journey she was on her second book with us, 'The magic of spirit'. The cards and first book had been mostly channelled through inspirational writing and telepathic thought guidance. When she started her second book with us, we guided her to use a Dictaphone on her phone. We chose to channel when she walked her dog Boyd, as his energy helped us to channel our words, and then Sharon would type it up on her computer. As we are channelling this book, it is all transmitting through telepathic communication, straight into the mind at a good pace. This is because Sharon's energies had risen and her trust in what she hears and sees in her mind has given us a clear channel. I mention this as we try to work with a lot of you in this way, and your acceptance and trust of us then accelerates our connection and is key to your ascension. Sharon has now written 9 books that are listed at the back of this book.

We carried on helping Sharon with her holistic business, bringing forth various ways to connect to people, such as phone and one-to-one readings. While all of this was going on in her life, her husband had another health scare and this prompted them to decide to sell their house, achieve better financial security to take off the pressure and enjoy life more. This was a planned move on her path, as we needed to shift her energy somewhere else to continue her spiritual work. She wrote out an affirmation to us; part of this was to ask for a short, stress-free house chain; a three or four bedroom house in a nice area, with good travel links, near dog walks, water and not too far from her children.

She put her trust out to us, and we worked behind the scenes to deliver what was needed for them. There was always the human ego doubt that would pop up in her mind so we also sent messages when she went to see a medium on platform. He brought Sharon's dad through, and after some great validation his message was about the move, that he was around helping in spirit, and all would be OK, and they would look back and know it was the best thing. He also said he saw a red 'sold' sign on the board. Sharon told her estate agent about this message and her face dropped, as they had just changed their blue sold signs to red that week.

Another sign we gave her was when she was clearing out their attic. Some of the items were from Chris's mum's and dad's house, so her thoughts were with them as they cleared those out. Sharon found one single old photo album in a box that had pictures of a holiday they took in the late 1980s in Canada. She was happy to remember how healthy and well they were back then and later on that day, she found some old video film; a couple of the clips were from that same holiday. Then at the end of the day, hidden behind all the boxes, she found a box she did not recognise, and she realised it was from Chris's mum's and dad's house. There was not much in it, just a couple of crystal vases and an old pickle tray. She put the glass dishes in the pickle tray and then tipped it upside down to see if it was marked metal on the base, and as she did this, we sent a coin, which fell onto the counter. It was a Canadian dollar! Sharon realised she had had three signs from us telling her that everything would be OK. I always felt amused when it clicked with her, and how she loved signs of clarity from us.

I saw that the move was quite an emotional time for all the human beings involved, and I can see why you say amongst yourselves that it's one of the most stressful things you can do. It's because of the human attachment to where you belong, the memories that you have built there, and the fear of what the future will hold. Sharon was also dealing with both her sons not living with them anymore, and as any parent who is close to their children will know, this is also quite an emotional time. These factors affect your energies, making them dip, so during Sharon's move we drew her back from working with spirit so much, keeping her development, but allowing everything else to stand still. She knew this was happening and accepted it.

Sharon and Chris felt very relieved when the move went well for them and they could relax. She continued with her wedding book business, which was doing well. We watched her channel her energy into landscaping her garden so she could have a place to sit and enjoy in the summer. This was good for Sharon, as she loves being outside and she was grounded with all this work, which helped her energies.

We also increased her spiritual work teaching and readings. While this was going on, Chris was struggling with his job and health and on Christmas Eve 2016 he was taken ill and lost more of his eyesight from a clot in the back of the eye. We have to admit this turned their lives upside down, for Chris especially, as this was his life path and was going to lead him to a spiritual path he had never foreseen. To reach this spiritual place he had to go through depression, acceptance and finding the inner strength to move forward with his life. Sharon also found this a hard time, seeing someone she loved suffering, while she tried to find the strength to move them both forward.

You remember that Chris was an artist, and when he became visually impaired he feared he would not be able to paint, but Sharon told him to put his trust in his guides. She was right, as we were ready to work with him, inspire him and connect him to spirit to bring loved ones forward through his art. He had been told of partially-sighted artists and researched their work, and this inspired him. So his journey began, and he told Sharon one day, *'I put the paint on the brush and don't know where it's going to go, and then I have painted something'*; this was the wisdom of his guides, leading him. His art changed and every piece now has a spiritual message that will have meaning and speak to people, because the pictures have a newfound spirit energy.

During this time, we led Sharon towards platform work. Her friend, an international medium, gave her a couple of opportunities at her shows to give messages that really helped Sharon's confidence. Then we led her to run spiritual church mediumship evenings at a community hall near her. I have to admit we were all getting very excited in spirit as this all took off. Meanwhile, when Sharon was giving readings at fairs, Chris had started doing sketches, picking up on their loved ones, and he then took this to the spiritual evenings with great results. This is work in progress with him, and we know as I write this that we are leading him to develop so we can strengthen our link with him. These two have a very interesting future ahead of them and we love to work with them both. Our main contact is going to be through the trance Sharon achieves, and we are focusing on bringing more ascension beings to her to learn from, and then she can take our messages out to others through her teaching.

Conclusion - I hope my story of this physical experience so far helps all of you who are light workers to understand how we help and work with you on your life's path. But remember, each experience will be different for you and us, as we are all unique individuals.

While we work with the star seed children to bring them into the love and light, there will also be life lessons for the human and spirit within to fulfil, as well as the ascension of that being. As in Sharon's case, I touched on parts of her life that affected the emotional wellbeing of the human form and spirit within to show how this affects the connection with us. I wanted to show the challenges we face as we work with you, and how sometimes the emotions can halt and delay your spiritual connection and development. We can 99.9.9% predict the human reactions on their path, but remember the example we gave of Sharon's postnatal depression. We cannot always anticipate how the human form will take an emotional upset; in this example we learnt that there were just too many things for a human to cope with all at once. But we adapt and have great patience in our existence; what might be five years to you is not measured in time by us, we are what we are, existing and knowing when the moment is right to continue. Also remember that the lessons Sharon learnt on her life's path so far have helped her with her mediumship and giving caring, loving messages of those we send to her, and through this she has deeper understanding of life. When we connect to you, we work with your mind's knowledge, experiences and emotions to give over the healing messages needed. We guide who comes to you for readings and healing, using your experience and energy to help you give the reading that is needed for that person.

Key to this journey is to TRUST. Trust your own first instincts and intuition as you walk your Earth's path and don't let your ego rule your head. Our fellow star ascension beings, and ourselves are here with unconditional love to help humanity find everlasting peace. I am just a very, very tiny part of this, but I know everything we do in the love and light helps you make a step forward in guiding you to what you could be and help you reach your full potential. You could be awesome beings, living on a nurtured, clean planet, helping and guiding each other to be the best you can be with no jealousy or resentment, just love, kindness, and the divine light of trust in the love and light.

Chapter 9

Discover your true self

Peace, light and unconditional love

The time has come for me to conclude this book and leave you a final message in these last few pages. I feel part of helping you learn is for you to reflect on this book and give you the space in this final chapter to reveal your thoughts and raise further questions to learn from. This will help you digest the knowledge these pages contain, and aid you to seek further knowledge and answers to your own questions. Remember you are here as a student from higher existence of ascension star beings, with a mission to complete on Earth. The missions will vary from gathering knowledge on a specific subject, to objective and learning lessons to help aid your own spiritual ascension.

Writing down your thoughts will help your understanding of what we have chosen to reveal to you all. We know your thoughts, but while you are in the restrictive third dimension energy matrix you need to process what you feel and your own thoughts to create greater understanding and clarity. This inner reflection will help you move forward on your life's spiritual path. When you have questions relating to these chapters, seek the answers from us and we will endeavour to answer them. We will lead you to what you need in books, the Internet, workshops and individuals that will help you. We will also appear in your dreams, and communicate through trance circles, mediums and healers. Remember that if you seek answers, you need to develop your inner unconditional love and prepare yourself to be able to receive them.

We ask you to take time with these questions and answer them at a steady pace with great reflection. Please do not skip this, as it is important for your own growth. You were led to this book, because you are at a stage in your spiritual growth where you can absorb its knowledge, which will be a trigger for further ascension development. To find your true self, you need to ask questions and seek answers, and in this way, you will find your true-life mission here on Earth.

So you understand why we set these questions, we have discovered in our own development that self-reflection is a sure way to inner and outer growth. In the third dimension restricted energy matrix it is easy for you to feel safe and not question the things you do not understand. You are afraid of change and that fear traps you in the third dimension energy grid. A lot of you do not question, and overlook the thoughts that tell you there is more to what you are now. Those who question and seek answers are the ones who grow, expand their minds and ascend. When you question, it raises your energies, which gives us the opportunity to work with you to shift you out of the third dimension rut you are stuck in.

We will be with everyone of you who reads these words. Your individual guides will bring back your written answers and thoughts to us and this will provide the knowledge we need to help you move forward on your Earth life's spiritual path.

What are your thoughts and understanding on being a multidimensional being living in a fifth dimensional existence?

Consider the ability to exist in the third dimension physical self, the fourth dimension astral self and the fifth dimension light body self – and beyond, all at the same time.

What are your thoughts and understanding of souls and higher selfs?

Reflect on the ascension levels, angels, guides and the role of the spirit within.

Do you believe in god?

Your understanding of god is our overseers, multidimensional beings existing in many dimension levels beyond your understanding. What are your thoughts on this statement?

Do you know your fifth dimensional mission while here on earth?

If the answer is NO, how do you think you can find out?

Do you feel you have been on Earth before, or in another physical existence on another planet, realm or dimension?

If YES, what is it that leads you to that conclusion? Do you remember your previous incarnations?

Have you had contact with star ascended beings – or as you call them, Aliens?

If YES, what was your experience and what have you learned from them?

How do you feel about your Mother Earth being a living entity?

Reflect here on the dark energies against the love and light energies in your world. Reflect on Mother Earth's ascension and your understanding of this. Also, ask yourself whether or not you feel she is fighting back against humanity's pollution.

What can YOU do to help your living planet heal and ascend so she can help humanity?

Remember she is a living entity with millions of years of history and a voice that we hear.

Do you believe in star people and a galactic group that works together to help humanity ascend?

Write down your thoughts and experiences and beliefs. If you believe in us, imagine what else there can be in the Universe.

Do you love yourself?

To find your true self and mission while here on Earth, loving yourself is key to this ascension. Acceptance of self and self-love is achieved by trusting you have great purpose, taking your attention to positive things in your life. Understanding your physical being and mind, you must get to know yourself before you can get to know your world and beyond.

What is the one thing you dream of doing in your life to bring you fulfilment?

Now think about what is stopping you and how you can make this dream your reality.

Here is an exercise for you to try to help raise your energies.

ATTENTION – practice taking your attention away from negative news feeds, social media and negative people you know.

Observe how you feel over a few weeks, and how this alters YOU, your energies and your perception of your world. Record the changes you observe below, to help with your development and future reflection.

For those of you that know you have had past life experiences, you will relate to this book and my experiences. Not all of humanity will have had a lot of past life experiences; some of you might be here for the first time. For those of you that are not sure, take a moment to ask yourself: do you have a repetitive dream? If yes, do you feel it's part of another existence, time and place? Do you have a health ailment that feels deep-set, which you struggle to deal with? Do you have fears or phobias, and you do not understand where they come from? We ask this as we have found in humans that you have the capability to pick up on the spirit within and previous physical experiences, and they manifest in your life without explanation or understanding on your part.

If you have the latter, my advice is to seek a past life regression specialist; they have wonderful ways to connect your past lives and help you heal so you can fulfil this mission on Earth. Now we could heal you, but we have found that these past life shadows which merge with the new spirit within are a great way for you to learn and find your spiritual path. Remember the example we gave as spirit within Sharon, which was her introduction to spirituality?

Through these chapters, I have touched on my physical connections in the third and fourth dimension energy frequencies. These you will know as past lives on Earth and other places. With the support of my fellow star ascension friends, my aim was to show you we are working with Mother Earth to help her ascension. We are encouraging a lot of spiritual writing at the moment in various degrees of written language for humanity to learn from. This is our way of making **first contact** with you all. We know that those who are led to these written works will take the newfound knowledge and it will help them on their life's mission.

It is a great time of change for humanity, and we know that at the moment, with the rising energies, a lot of you are struggling with the information flowing out to you from us. A lot of this information is coming through trance mediums, books and dreams. Remember the explanation of the three, four and five dimensions states. While in the three dimension your reality is restricted, by this we mean for example say your dream state and the knowledge we give you is as you know your reality, as you can not see beyond that. If you could see other worlds, dimensions and realms while on the earth plane your dreams would be come so different with all that new found knowledge and realities. Your thoughts could change your world and reality as you know it. As humanity ascends and your conscious mind expands this is what you will experience my friends in the future.

We ask you to trust your journey, and call your guides close to help you with this. You need to find your true self and you must be wondering, when will you know you have achieved this? I advise you to experience soul connection, learning to trust your intuition and learning to connect to the higher self. Our friend Sharon teaches this soul connection, when you experience this it will resonate deep within and bring light to your Earth path. Your energies will be the best they have been and you will be looking upon your fellow humanity and Mother Earth with great love and affection. When this happens, your Earth mission will simply flow, as your intuition, a gift from your spirit within, will be fully trusted. You will always know on your path, whenever something presents itself to you, whether it's wrong or right for you. To maintain the true self work on your meditation, link to your guides, higher self and inner spirit and you won't go wrong, my friends.

I now end this book by sending you unconditional love and blessings.

Ayderline xxxxxxx

About the Author

Sharon from Bengalrose Healing is a medium, author, holistic healer, spiritual teacher and mentor based in the United Kingdom.

Her book, *'Ayderline the Spirit Within'*, is part of a collection of books she has written. 'Utopia', *'The Magic of Spirit'*, 'The Magic of Words', *'Step into the Mind of a Medium'*, 'Heavenly Guidance', *'The light within Atlantis'*, 'New Earth - The light over the horizon', *'Your daily spiritual guidance diary'* and 'Inspiration Guidance Cards'.

Sharon is also the founder of the 'One Spiritual Movement' community www.onespiritualmovement.com
Facebook one spiritual movement

Sharon's books are available on Amazon and on her own website: www.bengalrose.co.uk.

Visit her website www.bengalrose.co.uk to find out more about Sharon and what she offers.

You can also find her on twitter @SBengalrose and FaceBook Bengalrosehealing.

Sharon has a YouTube channel with over one hundred fifty spiritual guidance videos. Search 'Sharon Bengalrose'.

Sharon also welcomes contact through
email: Sharon@bengalrose.co.uk

Printed in Great Britain
by Amazon